Voices
from the
Asylum

West Riding Pauper Lunatic Asylum

MARK DAVIS

WITH A FOREWORD BY NICCOLA SWAN
DIRECTOR, LEEDS MIND

AMBERLEY

Acknowledgements

Thanks go to the following people and organisations: Gary Brannan and all the staff at the West Yorkshire Archive Service located at Newstead Road, Wakefield, for all their support and assistance over the years; Gary Bouch, head of communications at Leeds and York Partnership NHS Foundation Trust, for his support and for allowing the use of the images from the medical casebooks; the Heritage Lottery Fund for their financial support; and to everyone who has supported 'The Friends of High Royds Memorial Garden' project from its conception. Proceeds for this book are going to High Royds Memorial Garden.

This book is dedicated to the memory of the 2,861 people buried at Buckle Lane Cemetery. May they rest in peace.

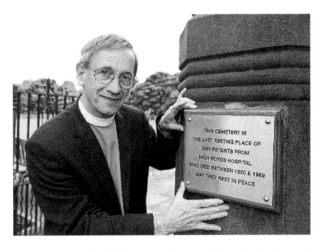

The Venerable David Lee, Archdeacon of Bradford, pictured at the thanksgiving service, September 2012.

Front cover: Emma Wigglesworth, who was admitted on 16 December 1910. Emma died at Menston on 12 January 1912.

First published 2013
Reprinted 2014

Amberley Publishing
The Hill, Stroud, Gloucestershire, GL5 4EP
www.amberley-books.com

Copyright © Mark Davis, 2013

The right of Mark Davis to be identified as the Author of this work has been asserted in accordance with the Copyrights, Designs and Patents Act 1988.

ISBN 978 1 4456 2173 9 (print)
ISBN 978 1 4456 2188 3 (ebook)

British Library Cataloguing in Publication Data.
A catalogue record for this book is available from the British Library.

Typesetting by Amberley Publishing.
Printed in Great Britain.

Foreword

I'm delighted that Mark has put together this further book, following on from his very successful earlier publication, *West Riding Pauper Lunatic Asylum.* That book recounted the overall story of the four locations from a number of different perspectives – the design, the construction, what has happened to the buildings subsequently, the managers and staff over the decades and, of course, the residents. This book focuses solely on this last group – the most important one. Simply and effectively, it shows us the faces and gives us a brief insight into the stories of thirty-seven of the people who were resident in Menston Asylum.

It is good that there is increasing interest in the old asylums, and this comes in part from people tracing their genealogy and family histories. Alongside this, there are many who want to understand what happened in these astonishing buildings and are curious about the care of people with mental ill-health over the centuries.

It is so important that we do not forget this essential part of our local history, and of the history of mental healthcare overall. It is essential that we remember the people for whom these extraordinary buildings had become home, many living there for almost all their lives, often without hope of release and not able to speak for themselves. We must respect their memories, and this book gives us insight into their individual stories, setting out the bare facts and ensuring that they are recorded and handed down. Mark's interest in miscarriages of justice and photography has combined to give us this very important document. It is vital that we understand how things were and how they have changed.

Things have moved on a great deal. Thank goodness, people with mental health problems are no longer treated like this. The stories recounted here are upsetting and we would be appalled at the thought that people could be deprived of their liberty, for sometimes very minor misdemeanours. While many dedicated healthcare professionals were doing their best, this is a history of injustice, abuse and denial of basic human rights.

On the Menston site, ordinary life has now been resumed, as families make their homes there in buildings that combine the old and the new. This book tells the stories of people long dead. But there are many people still alive today who used services at High Royds, often compelled to do so and detained against their will. Many were subjected to what we would now consider inhuman treatment, and some still pass the place with trepidation and terrible memories.

The quality of mental healthcare improves steadily, particularly as it is recognised that people with mental health problems often know best what sort of care will work for them. Increasingly, support from people who have had similar experiences is the most effective route. The existence of the asylums undoubtedly helped to foster negative views and attitudes. As these barriers are now broken down, people are becoming more willing to talk about their own experiences of being unwell, and thereby help others. Inappropriate attitudes to people with mental health problems can be challenged and people no longer need to be ashamed.

Nonetheless, people with mental health problems do still undoubtedly encounter stigma and discrimination. Campaigns like 'Time to Change' are critical in moving this on, and we are very fortunate that the NHS in Leeds has invested in it, with dedicated resource, and lots of activity. Helped by 'Time to Change' and other similar work, people can now openly challenge inappropriate views because people are no longer locked away in places like High Royds. Although people are, sadly, still detained ('sectioned'), there are legal provisions and checks to ensure they are not 'out of sight, out of mind', as so many of the people in this book were.

The Friends of High Royds Memorial Garden have secured funding and a great deal of local help, and have restored, and now maintain, the chapel and cemetery. In total, 2,861 people, like those featured in this book, found their final resting place here as their families did not claim their bodies. It is now a beautiful and moving place to go to contemplate these sad stories. Thank you, Mark, for enabling us all to read them.

Niccola Swan
Director, Leeds Mind
August 2013

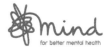

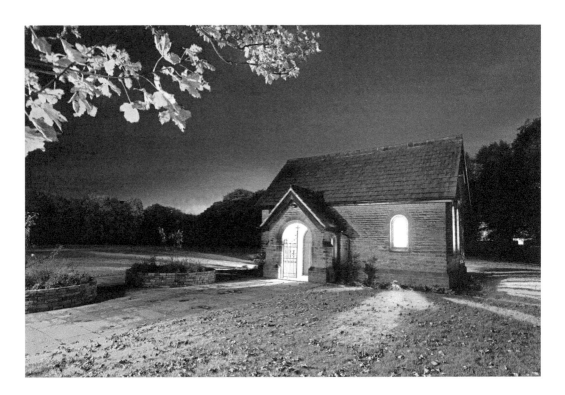

The Memorial Garden – March 2013.

Introduction

The voices of 'the apparent insane' who were admitted to the former pauper lunatic asylum at Menston are, for the most part, preserved in the original medical casebooks catalogued and stored at the West Yorkshire Archive Service in the unique collection identified as C485. Much of the material for the individual patients' stories has been sourced from the casebooks; other reference points include contemporary newspaper reports, asylum records and Ancestry Online.

The casebooks contain a wealth of information for both the historical researcher and the genealogist searching for relatives. Many of the terms used in these books are distinctly unsavoury by today's standards and expectations, but it is important that we understand that these descriptions and labels are historical and do not reflect modern-day treatment and principles. The study of the history of medicine, and more particularly that of psychiatry, often induces in the contemporary reader an understandable sense of relief that he or she is living in the modern world and not in the past. Yet the accounts of the patients in this book, representative of thousands of people admitted between 1888 (when the asylum opened on 8 October) and 1911 will resonate with all who take an interest in mental health today.

Patient confidentiality is protected by the '100-year rule' that limits access to records younger than a century to family members. Although data protection and confidentiality protect these former patients from exploitation, they do not silence them.

Within this book, the patients' voices are sometimes indirectly heard through the contents of doctors' certificates and clinical records, which have been summarised. More fascinating have been the direct reports of their speech, their letters (as well as those from relatives and friends) and, of course, those thought-provoking images, each individual picture giving us a window onto a unique human life. Every personal story in this book reaches out, not only to tell of mental distress, but of life outside the hospital, family, relationships and contemporary attitudes of a Victorian lunatic asylum and culture.

Under the Lunacy Act of 1845, to which all lunatic asylums were subject, patients had to be certified by two doctors, regardless of whether they had any experience in mental illness or not. Once admitted, the patient's physical state, mental condition and previous history were entered into the casebook. Over time, progress notes were added at regular intervals, as were charts, letters and sometimes pictures. The notes featured in this book were written by the medical staff: the medical superintendents, Dr John Greig McDowall (1888–November 1906) and Dr Samuel Edgerley (1906–December 1933), and the assistant medical officers, including Dr James R. Whitwell, Dr Richard Kirwan and Dr R. Clive Walker.

The majority of pauper insane patients admitted to Menston were direct transfers from the union workhouse, often referred to as the 'the Bastille' by the poor in the West Riding. The patients were certified by medical officers in the workhouse infirmary, where the selection process took place; others were sent at the direction of the criminal courts, having been certified as fit for removal by police doctors. The larger percentage of patients were of the pauper class who were regarded as insane, while a smaller percentage had become paupers as a result of their mental illness.

It is unfortunate that the medical records give very little information regarding physical and chemical treatments applied to individual patients. Of course, the fact that treatments are not mentioned does not mean that they were not employed – it may just mean the medical staff thought them not worthy of mention. Medical superintendent Dr Samuel Edgerley shed some light on the mysterious workings of the hospital in 1929 when discussing treatments with a newspaper reporter investigating claims of cruelty to patients. The superintendent was quite clear that in his thirty-two years of experience at Menston, there had not been one single instance of the straitjacket being deployed to restrain any patient. He went on to discuss the use of dangerous drugs and stated that only 3 grams of cocaine had been administered since 1921. Dr Edgerley maintained the principal drugs used were bromide and sleeping draughts, such as paraldehyde, used principally to quieten disruptive patients at night.

The thirty-seven patients who relate their stories in this book spent over 680 years between them under care and treatment. Many lived to a ripe old age, spending decades as inpatients, but for some life was decidedly shorter. It is a fact that in the early days around 90 per cent of deceased patients were subject to a post-mortem. The post-mortem was considered an important tool in understanding the cause and effect of mental illness, with emphasis on studying brain deformity and scar tissue.

Every patient within this book was laid to rest by the hospital authorities in land set apart on the south side of the hospital estate, situated at Buckle Lane. The 2-acre site, complete with a mortuary chapel, was drained and laid out in 1890 specifically to bury the unclaimed asylum dead. There are many reasons to justify why families did not collect their relatives' remains, among them poverty, the stigma of having a relative in the asylum and, sadly, that some patients had quite literally been forgotten by their family through the sheer passage of time. The cemetery opened on 3 December 1890, at which time Sarah Ann Walker, aged forty-five, was laid to rest. When the cemetery eventually closed on 14 January 1969 upon the funeral of Alice Maud Wardman, aged ninety, a total of 2,861 people had already been interred over the seventy-nine years of operational use.

Contrary to various legends, the funeral service in the early days, although basic, was dignified; the coffin was of plain deal pine and the burial service brief, more often than not with only the grave digger and clergy in attendance. Patients were initially interred singularly, but were in later years buried three deep, with only a cast-iron marker denoting the grave and row number.

The names of patients whose stories and accounts appear in this book have not been altered or changed. By giving the patients their true names, we rescue their cases from being discussed impassively as no more than examples of Victorian and Edwardian asylum diagnosis and treatment. The stories, however, do not provide the last word on any of these people; they only represent a snapshot of a time when the individuals were undergoing extreme human distress. As I have been researching and compiling this book, I have often wondered how the lives of these patients might have turned out had modern care and treatments been available.

Through this book we can correctly attribute personal lives and experiences, and make their voices count for something. They can educate us all so that we can make sure the mistakes of the past are never repeated. The voices of these people deserve to be heard.

Despite being firmly in the twenty-first century, the fear and stigma associated with mental illness unfortunately still remains, although campaigns like 'Time to Change' work tirelessly towards breaking down these barriers.

Mark Davis
August 2013

Care and Treatment

After years of construction, the new asylum at Menston was to take in its first thirty female inmates on 8 October 1888; all were transfers from the overcrowded Wadsley Asylum in Sheffield. The first patient to be entered into the casebook was Elizabeth Johnson, who spent sixteen years at the hospital, dying on 15 February 1904; she was subsequently laid to rest at the asylum cemetery at Buckle Lane. The first sixty-one admissions were all female. It would be November 1888 before the male patients began to arrive, again transfers from Wadsley. Like the women, many had already spent a considerable time in West Riding asylums prior to arriving at Menston and were, in the main, wretched and worn out. The majority of these early admissions were destined to live out their years in the asylum receiving palliative care. Patients were strictly segregated by their sex, the male population occupying a collection of pavilions to the left of the administration building, which was mirrored on the female side. Further segregation included the epileptics, the acute and recent cases, the sick and infirm, and the chronically ill.

In those early days, the hospital was known as the West Riding Pauper Lunatic Asylum, Menston. By the 1920s, the asylum had been renamed Menston Mental Hospital, before eventually gaining the title 'High Royds Psychiatric Hospital' in 1963. When ultimate closure came in February 2003, the former asylum was one of the last surviving hospitals of its kind to be still functioning. The asylum has been described as possibly the most magnificent example of J. Vickers Edwards' architecture, and could certainly stake a claim to be the finest example of the broad arrow corridor system. At one time, the sprawling institution boasted a library, a fully equipped surgery, a fully stocked dispensary, a large ballroom, a butcher, a baker, and even its own linked railway. The addition by the 1930s of a sweetshop, cobbler, upholsterer and tailor, completed what was really in effect a self-contained village for the mad.

To be admitted to a lunatic asylum in the nineteenth century was fraught with danger, and certainly for some, the beginning of what was in effect an arbitrary life sentence on a locked ward. It is certainly true that as the asylums filled to capacity with the human wreckage of the newly industrialised society, the emphasis was on containment, management and administration. The downward spiral for many people saw them admitted to the workhouse, the asylum or prison. Some of the people who voice their stories in this book found themselves in all three.

Although discharge rates were quoted up to 50 per cent, it was not enough to be relieved or recovered if there was no home for the patient to return to. If family were not available to take in the convalescent, then they would remain in the asylum. There are also recorded instances of patients remaining under care and treatment at Menston when relieved, simply because they were extremely useful. As an example, one male patient from Knaresborough superintended a building project while a female from the same workhouse union was placed in charge of the hospital sewing room.

The supposed cause of insanity and how that cause manifested itself could be worlds apart; for example, a patient of whose affliction was supposedly caused by milk fever might display the Victorian favourite, 'mania' (to rage furiously). A popular misconception is the belief that unmarried mothers were admitted to the asylum purely because they were pregnant. The reality is somewhat different – unmarried mothers were admitted, but only if they were suffering from a mental illness. The Mental Deficiency Act of 1913 brought in legislation to categorise women who repeatedly had children out of wedlock as feeble-minded and send them to the mental deficiency colony, and not the lunatic asylum.

There were a multitude of reasons for being admitted to the asylum: religious frenzy, bad luck, or disappointment in love, reading too much poetry, intemperance, sexual frenzy, and dementia, to name a few. Once admitted, rules were applied. Within seven days after the reception of a patient, the medical casebook had to be filled in with the following particulars, as required in 1895:

A statement of the name, age, sex, previous occupation of the patient, whether married, single, or widowed, and a copy of the statement of facts contained in the medical certificates accompanying the reception order.

An accurate description of the external appearance of the patient upon admission: of the habit of body, and temperament; appearance of the eyes, expression of countenance, and any peculiarity in form of head; physical state of the vascular and respiratory organs, and of the abdominal viscera, and their respective functions; state of the pulse, tongue, skin, etc.; and the presence or absence, on admission, of bruises or other injuries.

A description of the phenomena of the mental disorder: the manner and period of the attack, with a minute account of the symptoms, and the changes produced in the patient's temper or disposition; specifying whether the malady displays itself by any, and what, delusions, or irrational conduct, or morbid or dangerous habits or propensities; whether it has occasioned any failure of memory or understanding; or is connected with epilepsy, or ordinary paralysis, or general paralysis.

Every particular which can be obtained respecting the previous history of the patient: what are believed to have been the predisposing and exciting causes of the attack; what were the previous habits, whether active or sedentary, temperate or otherwise; whether the patient has experienced any former attacks and, if so, at what periods; whether any relatives have been subject to insanity or other nervous diseases, or phthisis; whether the present attack was preceded by any, and what, premonitory symptoms; and whether the patient has undergone any, and what, previous treatment, or has been subjected to restraint of personal liberty.

Subsequent entries describing the course and progress of the case, and recording the medical and other treatment, with the results, shall be made in the casebook for patients at the times herein-after mentioned, that is to say: once oftener when necessary; afterwards, in recent or curable cases, once at least in every month, and in chronic cases, subject to little variation, once in every three months. But all special circumstances affecting the patient, including seclusion and mechanical restraint, and all accidents and injuries, must be at once recorded. A printed copy of this, and the last preceding, rule shall be inserted at the beginning of every casebook for patients.

Routine in the Asylum

When Nurse Gwen Hartley, who started her career at the hospital in 1924, gave her memoirs to the local newspaper in 2002, she recalled how she would have to scrub half the mosaic floor with six patients from her ward. She also remembered how after breakfast she had to round up patients, pick up two buckets and go through the backyard to where the coal was dropped off, before carrying it back to the wards to light the fires. The wards had stone floors, which she and six patients had to scrub with soap. Patients were bathed once a week and had their hair and nails cut. The wards were heated by coal fires and were lit by gas lamps. At mealtimes, three patients would be taken to the kitchen and would then have to push a trolley of food back to their ward. The furniture in the wards was both heavy and dark, and the dormitories were packed tight with beds, without any space even for a bedside cabinet. Gwen experienced numerous incidents of patients escaping, despite the complex having tight security with every door locked after a nurse entered or left a room. The windows on the wards only opened by 2 inches and some patients would use the spoons to try and unscrew the windows to escape. The hospital took a guinea out of Gwen's wages for living accommodation. All nurses were expected to live in-house until they had been there three years, and were not allowed to marry.

Entertainment for the patients included dances each Friday night in the magnificent ballroom where the male and female population were allowed to mix, under the watchful eye of the nurses and attendants. The social event of the year was the annual asylum ball, held just after Christmas with around 800 dancers taking part. Magnificent decorations, which took weeks to prepare and arrange, included brightly coloured festoons and tinsel draped overhead and along the walls. In 1924, the valuable addition of a projector enabled the showing of silent movies. Where possible, the patient population was encouraged to work, which was viewed as a valuable aid to recovery.

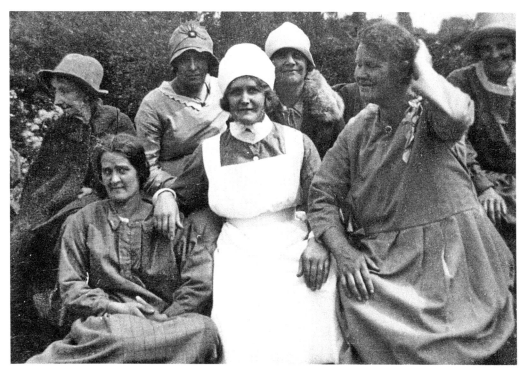

Pictured here in the early twentieth century is Nurse Isabella Duesberry with her charges.

The Memorial Garden, Buckle Lane

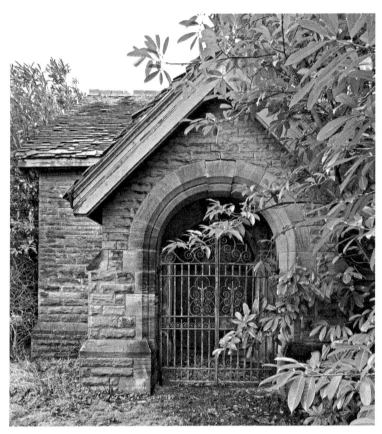

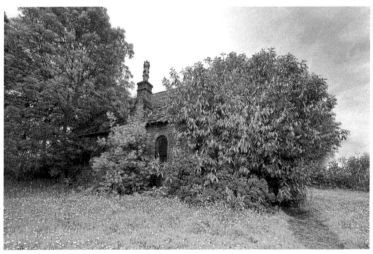

The mortuary chapel and cemetery prior to restoration, September 2008.

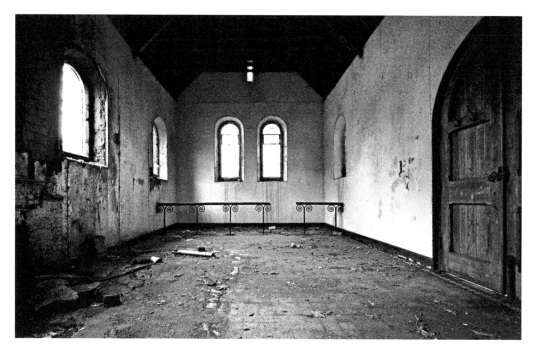

In 2008, the Friends of High Royds Memorial Garden was formed. The aim of the group was to restore the former asylum cemetery and mortuary chapel, which had remained neglected for many years. Through the assistance of both organisations and individuals, we have been able to bring both dignity and a voice to those long-forgotten people interred there. In 2013, the little cemetery is a haven of peace and tranquillity where we can reflect upon the lives of the people who found their last resting place here. All the men, women and children buried in unmarked graves at Buckle Lane have one thing in common; they all died alone, without anyone to mourn their passing or collect their mortal remains.

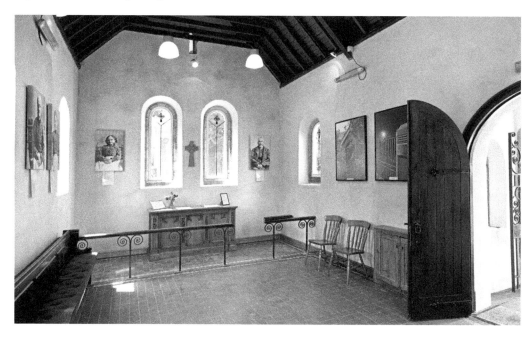

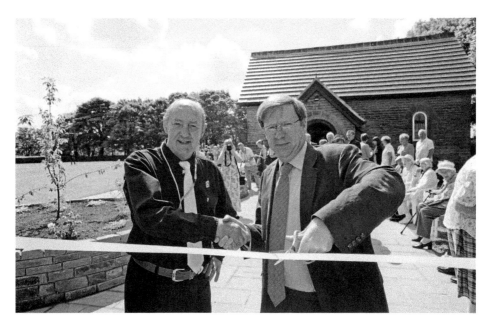

The restoration of the Memorial Garden was originally the brainchild of Derek Hutchinson (pictured, above left, with Paul Farmer, chief executive officer of Mind), the late John Steel OBE, former secretary, and Ron Sweeney, the current chairman and trustee of the friends of the High Royds Memorial Garden, who is pictured below left, with Mark Davis, author of this book. Ron has some thirty years' experience as a volunteer in the mental health sector, and ran the Windmill Club and Drop-In Centre to assist patients from High Royds, and other areas. Building on his experience and academic studies, he is preparing a doctoral thesis, based on *Voices from the Past*, as to how best to reach out to and help those with mental health issues now that the emphasis is on 'Care in the Community'.

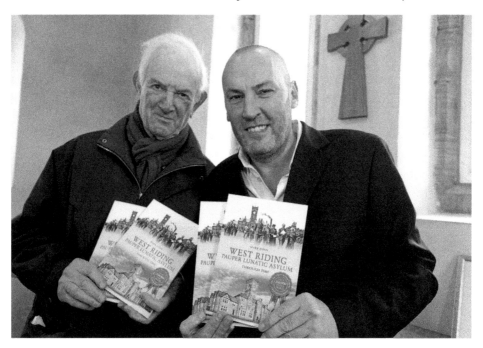

The Two Thousand, Eight Hundred and Sixty One

We were the unknown, the nothing, the nameless
We were the discarded, agonising remnants
Of a society that was too busy to grant any of us empathy
Or treat us with any dignity in the time of our demise

We were the unfortunate, the awkward, the taboo of our time
We were the mentally retarded, the social undesirables
We laid here in the soil and meant absolutely nothing to you
We were the two thousand, eight hundred and sixty one

Then recently, apparently, someone made the choice quite rightly
To do something about our non-consensual vow of eternal silence
Now a chapel and garden, alive and new
Stand proud upon the ground once used to bury our memory forever

We will be the known, the something, at last the named
We will be recognised as an agonising tragedy
Of a society that was once too busy to grant any of us empathy
Now we will be something more than the two thousand, eight hundred and sixty one

And so to all of you, the friends we never knew

Thank you.
David J. Lynch (2013)

...ty of fetid pus evacuated
...remication wit necrosed bone —
...ient was this morning confin...
...d — She is much exhausted
...ess of semi-delirious — The
...all feeble of the subject of
...tient has all the symptoms of
... is very exhausted of incline...
...d delirious — She is getting
...eatment local & general wit
... stimulants —
...atient gradually sank & died

Died December 29 – 1890

Cause of Death — Puerperal Septicæmia

Emma Appleyard

Number of admission: 935
Occupation: Housewife.
Admitted: 8 December 1890.

Facts observed: Refused to take food, inability to recognise husband.
Other facts communicated: Barbara Jessie Cloudsley Hunter, Nurse General Infirmary, Leeds, informs me that Emma Appleyard never asks for a bed pan but passes her motions into bed.
Age: Twenty-five.
Religious persuasion: Salvation Army.

History: Has been in Leeds Union Infirmary for a week for 'abscess in cheek'. Is pregnant, has one child aged sixteen months old and after its birth was mentally afflicted for some weeks but was treated at home. No family history of insanity, phthisis or intemperance. Husband thinks that patient has dreaded her approaching confinement and this has, in his opinion, led to present attack.

Diagnosis: Melancholic, pregnancy.
Causation: Ill Health, Pregnancy.
Prognosis: Doubtful if somewhat grave.

When Emma was admitted to Menston Asylum in 1890 she was described as 'a short, fairly well nourished woman of weak, anaemic, cachectic appearance'. Attempts to engage her in conversation were futile, with the exception of Emma stating her age. It would appear from her limited notes that her breakdown came about as a result of her fear of giving birth, which occurred on 23 December 1890 when she delivered a male child. The child was both small and feeble, and unfortunately the subject of spina bifida. He died on 28 December. Emma soon developed Puerperal Septicaemia and died at 10.30 p.m. on 29 December.

Although only in Menston for a month, no one collected her remains and she was laid to rest along with her son, James, on 5 January 1891 at Buckle Lane Cemetery, row 9, grave 21.

Emma and her son were the third and fourth patients to be buried in the newly opened cemetery.

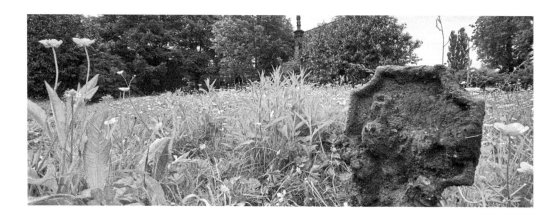

'Says he has been tortured for twenty-two years, his food has been poisoned and interfered with'

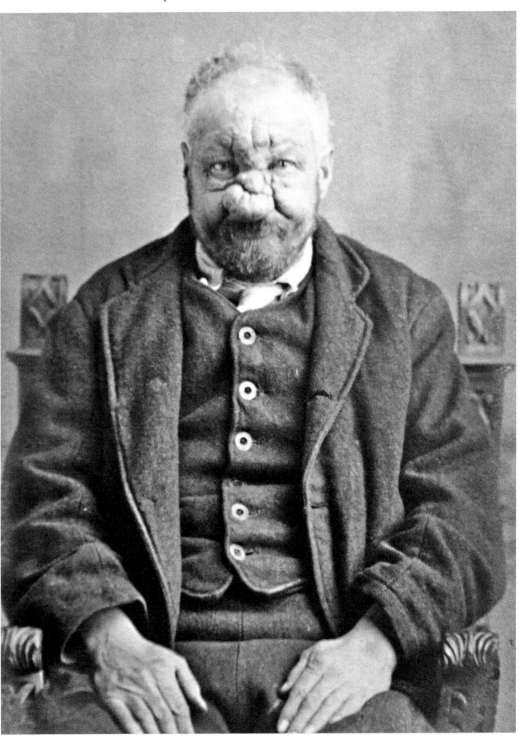

Thomas Edmondson

Number of admission: 229

Admitted: 1 March 1889.

Age: Thirty-one.

Age on first attack: Thirty.

Religious persuasion: Church of England.

Married, single or widowed: Single.

Occupation: Bricklayer.

Chargeable to: Bradford Union Workhouse.

Previous place of abode: Bradford

Relieving officer: Robert Garnett.

Name and residence of nearest known relative: Barbara Edmondson (mother), 18 Elsworth Street, Bradford.

Facts observed by W. S. Proctor, Bradford: Has various delusions that he has done something wrong when in 'India' and that now he is persecuted by the neighbours for what he has done wrong. That the neighbours are set to persecute him by the government, and that his food and drink are poisoned too.

Other facts communicated: Barbara Edmondson (mother) reports that the patient, her son, has been wrong since Christmas, that he has delusions that he is to be poisoned and refuses his food. That he is sleepless at nights, that he is violent and threatens to murder his mother.

Mental state: Patient begins by informing us that he has other names, Luchmond Dass, Mahomet Falier and Thomas Edmondson, the first two represent girls who have tortured him, the other is an foreign name and he says is only 'skin deep'. He is most irrational and deluded, aggressive and irritable. Says he has been tortured for twenty-two years, his food has been poisoned and interfered with. He can give a fair amount of his life, but his whole train of thought is irrational and delusional.

Suicidal: Yes.

Dangerous to others: Yes.

Diagnosis: Delusional Insanity.

Causation: Syphilis.

Prognosis: Unfavourable.

Regarded as a dangerous and irritable man, Thomas's prognosis was unfavourable. Thomas talked passionately of his fear of electricity and worried that his body and soul were about to be destroyed by some means. He also believed that his family had already been murdered by doctors. The medical staff noted in his casebook that he believed himself to be the Rajah and that his whiteness was only skin deep, he feared being attacked by European white men. Over time, Thomas retained both his delusions and excitement, ensuring he received end of life care. When he died aged seventy-one he had spent thirty-nine years at Menston.

He was buried at Buckle Lane Cemetery on 22 February 1928, row 24, grave 4.

Name *Hilda Butler*

Occupation *None*

Admitted on the

Facts observed by *John Sykes Grad. in*
Constant restlessness, walking a
to destroy everything she come
talk distinctly & generally de

Other facts communicated :
Her mother informs me that
much as she will throw Knive
throw. She will sit on the f
sleeple

Hilda Butler

Number of admission: 597
Admitted: 13 January 1890.
Age: Four.
Previous place of abode: Brook Street, Cleckheaton.

Facts observed: Constant restlessness, walking aimlessly about and attempting to destroy everything she comes in contact with. Unable to talk distinctly and generally defective mentally.

Other facts communicated: Her mother informs me that she is dangerous to those about her in as much as she will throw knives or scissors or anything that she may find at them. She will sit on the fire; in fact the fire has an attraction for her. She is very sleepless and is convulsed every night.

History: Patient was first observed to have fits when about five months old and they have gradually become stronger. She was born in Africa. Her parents support that the condition may have been caused by the hot climate or a sunstroke – when an infant in arms. No family history bearing on the case.

Mental state: Patient is a bright, good-tempered child. Appears to have some intelligence but does not speak intelligibly – recognises a watch and tries to open it – but does not name it. Mischievous and impulsive in her actions.

Physical condition: A well-developed, pleasant-looking child.

Diagnosis: Imbecility & Epilepsy.
Causation: Congenital, Sunstroke.
Prognosis: Unfavourable.
Treatment: Palliative.

It is clear when little Hilda was admitted to Menston the prognosis was not good. However, by early January 1890 she was noted to be happy and contented, having made friends in the ward and was learning nursery rhymes. As January drew to a close she took a turn for the worse, with her fits becoming more frequent and a rapid loss of weight. Hilda's notes of 15 June 1891 state: 'Almost a skeleton, cannot long sustain, unable to take nourishment', and she passed away on 17 June. Sadly, aged just six, nobody came forward to collect her remains and she was laid to rest at the hospital cemetery, Buckle Lane Cemetery, 22 June 1891, row 9, grave 39.

'Has had a rather hard time of it when he could get no work'

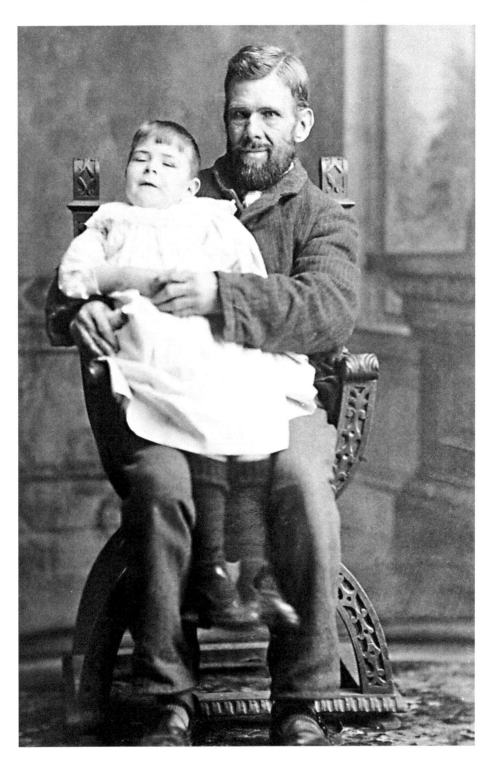

George Brown

Number of admission: 3145
Admitted: 24 April 1896.
Chargeable to: Keighley.
Age: Forty-four.
Married, single or widowed: Married.
Occupation: Chimney Sweeper.
Religious persuasion: Church of England.
Previous place of abode: Workhouse.
Asylum: Has not been in any asylum.
Relieving Officer: J. Williston.
Name of nearest known relative: Maria E. Brown (wife), inmate of Keighley Workhouse.

Facts observed by W. L. Gabriel, Keighley: He talks excitedly about various fancied grievances in a round about manner, attempts to explain his reasons for having attempted to create a disturbance earlier in the day. His statements were disconnected and showed a mark of intelligence.

Other facts communicated: The Workhouse Master states that he made his escape over a wall this morning and went down to the office of the clerk to the guardians, where he told excitedly, in a threatening manner, of his removal by a policeman to the workhouse.

Mental state: Patient goes into conversation readily but talks in a somewhat foolish fashion. He relates a lot of imaginary wrongs which he suffered from the guardians while at the workhouse, namely that when he could get work they would not let him out to take it, this led to acts of excitement and violence, on one occasion he took off one of his clogs and threw it at someone and another time he got over the wall and escaped from the institution. When asked why he ever got into the workhouse, he explains but the explanation is involved and unsatisfactory. He quite recognises his condition and position and states that he has always been steady and a moderate drinker. Has had rheumatic fever about five years ago. Has had a rather hard time of it when he could get no work, as his wife was not able to do anything to help in getting a living.

Dangerous to others: Yes.
Insane: One year.
Supposed cause: Not known.

The image of George shows him to be holding a small child, although the child is not named. I believe the child to be Ethel Wilson, though why they were photographed together is a mystery. Throughout his time at Menston, George worked in the wards, gardens and on the hospital farm, and though described as a good worker was also deemed to be quarrelsome, emotional and at times violent towards other patients. One thing George maintained throughout was his grievance towards the union workhouse for his incarceration. After nine years as a patient, George died of valvular heart disease on 1 August 1905, aged fifty-three. He was buried at Buckle Lane Cemetery on 4 August 1905, row 7, grave 3.

'She exhibits a certain amount of intelligence'

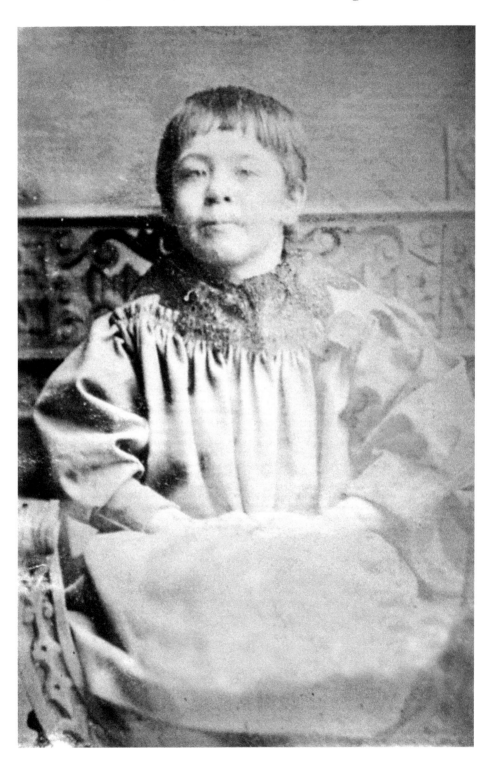

Ethel Wilson

Number of admission: 2290

Admitted: 10 January 1895.

Chargeable to: Bradford.

Age: Six.

Age on first attack: Birth.

Religious persuasion: Church of England.

Previous place of abode: Bradford Union Workhouse.

Name of nearest known relative: Father, John Wilson, 3 Jackson Street, Bradford.

Relieving Officer: W. M. Parker.

Facts observed by H. B. Procter: This is an idiot apparently from birth, is very mischievous and will attack anyone that is near her, will scratch them, kick them and bite them.

Other facts communicated: Kay Good, nurse, reports that she is very troublesome and requires a great deal of attention, also that she is very vicious, mischievous, that she bites, scratches and attacks other patients.

Mental state: Patient is a child where appearances suggest mental defect, but is not characteristically idiotic. She is able to articulate perfectly and can readily carry on a little conversation. She knows where she is, whence she came, has some little idea of the meaning of her position. She exhibits a certain amount of intelligence. In a general way she does not possess much knowledge, being unable to identify coins or recognise letters of the alphabet. In addition to much mental defect as has been noted, she exhibits deluded mental behaviour. Having examination without provocation bites and scratches those around her, after this she becomes emotional and seems to understand that she has given way to uncontrollable persons and subsequently will give one the impression that she is capable of exercising more affection.

Ethel was the daughter of a plasterer from Bradford and the eldest child of the family, having a sister Annie just one year younger. Although her reception notes clearly label her an 'idiot', it was noted in 1898 'that her intelligence being little less than that of an ignorant child of her years'. Regardless of the fact, Ethel by modern day standards should not have been institutionalised. She remained at the asylum until her death in 1915, aged twenty-six.

She was buried at Buckle Lane Cemetery on 7 May 1905, row 2, grave 29, after twenty years at Menston Asylum.

Dear. Father April 3rd 1893 and Mother I write these few lines to you hoping that you are both well has it leaves me very well at present you must let me now how Sister Ellen. his getting on in Australia. I Should never have been where I am If my Father had been kind to me when I was younger. Dear Mother Don't Fret over me. I have been troubled a great Deal over those men that brought me to mension has they was riding along the road with me. they begun to ask me Several Question about one place and then another. and they got from one word from another. Oh dear Mother God nows all. and all things works together for good.

Jonas Pearson

Number of admission: 1721

Admitted: 16 March 1893.

Age: Thirty.

Age on first attack: Thirty.

Chargeable to: Bierley Union Workhouse Bradford.

Religious persuasion: Protestant.

Married, single or widowed: Single.

Occupation: Weaver.

Asylum: Has not been in any Asylum.

Relieving Officer: H. Herdson.

Name and residence of nearest known relative: William Pearson (father), 1 Cooper Lane, Bradford.

Relatives similarly affected: Sister.

Facts observed by J. Logaw, Wibsey: Says that he is being slowly but surely poisoned through his food, being constantly tampered with, that he is always being pursued by enemies and that he went out to the fields this morning and searched for his money.

Other facts communicated: His mother informs me that for some time he has been very strange in his ways, that for whole nights he has kept praying and shouting at the pitch of his voice.

Insane: Five days.

Supposed cause: Not known.

Business Anxieties: Yes.

Overwork: Yes.

Fevers: Yes.

Pictured are pages one and two (see pages 24 and 26) of a heart-rending letter written, but never posted, by Jonas to his mother and poultry dealer father on 3 April 1893, just weeks after his reception into Menston. The letter addressed to both parents is clearly written for his mother Bridget's attention, given the fact his father was blind from birth, and gives us an insight into the despair he was feeling at the time. Jonas, one of eight children, was to spend twelve years under the banner of 'care and treatment', during which he persistently had auditory and visual hallucinations, mostly involving his grandmother watching and following him. Employed usefully in the ward and scullery, he remained, up until his death on 4 May 1905 of heart disease in deep depression and, in the opinion of the medical staff, suicidal.

He was buried at Buckle Lane Cemetery on 10 May 1905, row 6, grave 11, aged forty-two.

I am as incent has the lambs in the fields. and has armless. I hope I shall son be at home with you again I will honour and obey you all the days of my life. I feel a lot better in my mind. so good night you now I can't help People saying wrong things about me I have worked hard to save what I have I have been very careful Dear mother I do wish I was set free God nows I am in the right to serve him he his over us all. so good night to you all.

Dear mother I have left to God to make the man come unto to him it his very hard to be in a Place like mine. I remain yours
     truly loving son
   Jonas Pearson. x x x x x x x x x
x x x x x x me x x x x may God Bless those that sets free no Place home his swet there is

April 3rd 1893

Dear Father and Mother Turite these few lines to you hoping that you are both well has it leaves me very well at present you must let me now how Sister Ellen his getting on in Australia. I should never have been where I am If my father had been kind to me when I was younger. Dear Mother Don't Fret over me. I have been troubled a great Deal over those men that brought me to mension has they was riding along the road with me, they begun to ask me Several Questions about one place and then another. and they got from one word from another. Oh dear Mother God nows all and all things works together for good.

I am has inecent has a Child about what they have tried to bring on Me about 2 children they say I have murdered and before we reach mension They Pointed to a wood near Leeds as if I had done the crime. Dear Mother IHave been a little wild with myself but never moment have I taken any childs life. God made us every one. I have good meals to eat but plain, you must let Me now if brother Edwin as got any work. But I must Conclude I have not time to write any more Present Tsend my best love to you all, and all my friends and Relations, and tell them to write to me, and you must and see one and you must bring some off my friends with you. God is good and his mercy endured forever

I am as inecent as the lambs in the fields and has armless. I hope I shall soon be at home with you again I will honour and obey you all the days of my life. I feel a lot better in my mind. So good night you now I can't help people saying wrong things about me I have worked hard to save what I have I have been very careful

Dear mother I do wish I was set free god nows I am in the right to Serve him he his over us all. so good night to you all. Dear mother I have left to God to make the man come unto him it his very hard to be in a place like mine.

I remain yours

truly loving son

Jonas Pearson x x x x x x x x x x may god Bless x x x x

those that set me free

home is sweet there

is no place like it

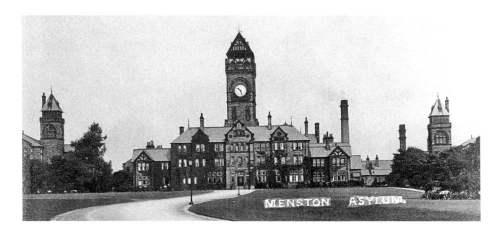

'Patient has delusions that she has been given poison'

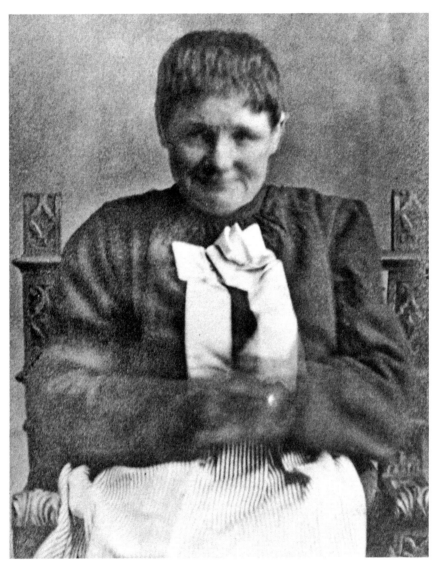

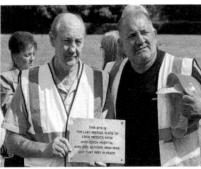

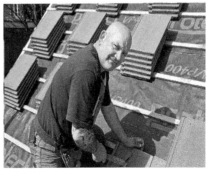

Cecily Sedgwick

Number of admission: 2717
Admitted: 29 July 1895.
Age: Twenty-eight.
Age on first attack: Twenty-eight.
Married, single or widowed: Married.
Religious persuasion: Catholic.
Occupation: Housewife.
Chargeable to: Bradford.
Previous place of abode: Bradford Union Workhouse.
Nearest known relative: W. J. Sedgwick (husband), Bradford.
Relatives similarly affected: Not known.
Children: Three.
Relieving Officer: J. Maudsley.

Insane: One week.
Supposed cause: Not known.
Dangerous: Is dangerous to others.

Facts observed by W. B. Procter: She is really quite insane and restless, and that she walks around in an insane manner. She is also so full of delusions that she sees her husband on the wall and talks to him saying that she has had poison given to her by a woman.

Other facts communicated: Mr Sedgwick (husband) reports that she wanders about at night and day, and that she has delusions that she has been given poison, that her friends are her enemies and also that her neighbours are her enemies, she thinks that they are bewitching her, he says that she is dangerous to others.

Cecily was admitted directly from the Bradford Union Workhouse Infirmary. Her husband, Mr Sedgwick, reported at the time of her admission auditory and visual illusions and restlessness. She was convinced poison had been administered to her by a woman and also imagined seeing her husband on the wall. Initially, Cecily was quiet and manageable, even being placed on work detail in the laundry. However, on 1 April 1898 she was transferred to the female chronic block when her mental health deteriorated.

Cecily was to spend fifty-nine years at Menston Asylum, eventually dying in 1954, having seen two World Wars pass as she remained under care and treatment.

The Buckle Lane Cemetery is home to many, many people who, like Cecily, spent half a century or more at Menston. We give thanks to her great-grandson Alan Storey for his devotion in restoring the mortuary chapel roof to the memory of the Nan he never knew. Alan is pictured left.

Cecily was buried on 20 February 1954, row 9, grave 28. She shares her grave with Daniel Barker, aged forty-four, buried in 1891; Margaret Foster, aged sixty-eight, buried in 1928; and Gertrude Flanders, aged eighty-seven, buried in February 1954.

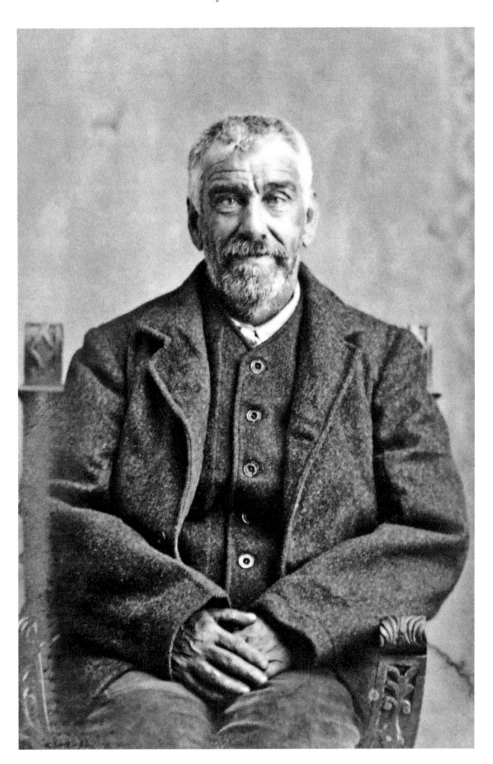

John Constantine

Number of Admission: 328
Admitted: 10 May 1889.
Age: Twenty-eight.
Age on first attack: Ten.
Religious persuasion: None.
Married, single or widowed: Single.
Occupation: None.
Chargeable to: Ripon.
Previous place of abode: Ripon Union Workhouse.
Name and residence of nearest known relative: John Constantine (father), Stonebridge Gate, Ripon.

Facts observed by T. I. Frankland M.R.C.S., Ripon, 19 June 1872: Wild excitable manner, I cannot judge by conversation as he is deaf and dumb, but his actions are quite inconsistent with a sane state of mind.

Other facts communicated: The mother says she is unable to manage him and that he often gets into danger.

History: A transfer from the North Riding Asylum into which he was admitted upon a certificate dated 19 June 1872.

Mental state: Patient is a deaf mute – he appears to have some appreciation of what is said to him and makes a hopelessly unintelligible attempt at articulation – becoming quite animated – appears happy – is not objectionable.

Supposed cause: Not known.
Epileptic: Not.
Suicidal: Not.
Dangerous to others: At times.

Although John was admitted to Menston in 1889, he was a transfer from the North Riding Asylum where he had been since June 1872, when admitted as a young boy aged just ten. John, of Irish descent, was both deaf and dumb from birth, which his father, a labourer, failed to state on the 1871 census. The casebooks indicate he was reduced mentally, yet he managed to work on the farm unsupervised for many years quite cheerfully. Understanding what was said to him, others could not, rendering derogatory labels such as 'Dummy Patient' and 'A Fairly Good Imbecile' quite common. He would make an effort to speak, which was noted in the casebook as 'rather amusing to observe'.

John passed away in March 1927 aged sixty-five. He was buried at Buckle Lane Cemetery on 16 March 1927, row 28, grave 11, following fifty-five years of care and treatment.

'Laundress of Workhouse says she threatened her with a ladling can'

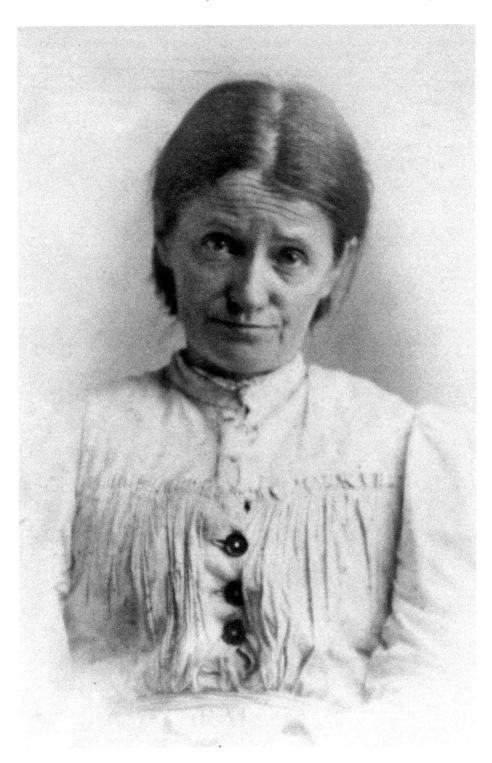

Elizabeth Ann Beecroft

Number of admission: 4332

Admitted: 10 September 1898.

Age: Forty-four.

Age on first attack: Forty.

Religious persuasion: Church of England.

Married, single or widowed: Single.

Occupation: Cotton winder.

Chargeable to: Skipton.

Previous place of abode: 14 Mill Bridge.

Nearest known relative: E. Beecroft (sister), Mill Gill, Gargrave.

Asylum: Menston.

Relieving Officer: W. Green.

Insane: One month.

Attack: Second.

Supposed cause: Not Known.

Epileptic: Not.

Suicidal: Not.

Dangerous to others: Not.

Facts observed by J. Readman: She is a certified imbecile, told me she was pregnant and that when the baby arrives she will have heaps of money. She says she has four babies. She is incoherent in her language.

Other facts communicated: Laundress of workhouse says she threatened her with a ladling can and that she is always rambling in her talk, talking about babies.

When Elizabeth, a former cotton spinner, was admitted to Menston Asylum in September 1898, it was for the second and last time. Despite her notes stating she is a certified imbecile, she had in fact held down a job while living with her parents, William and Ann, in Gargrave, North Yorkshire. Once back in Menston there was little hope, her prognosis was unfavourable and her treatment palliative. Just six months before her death, one of the last comments reads 'Jan 31 1908: A dirty, demented patient. She cannot be employed and requires a great deal of attention'. Sadly, when death came, both her parents were dead and her siblings failed to collect her remains.

Elizabeth was laid to rest at Buckle Lane Cemetery on 21 July 1908, row 15, grave 4, aged fifty-four, after ten years in Menston Asylum.

James Rhodes

Feb. 23 date. 1895.

Brothers

Sir

Joseph Rhodes.

I write to you hoping to find you and
my Brother Sir Joshua - and all Brothers
and Sisters and all your family's in Good
health has it Leaves me at Present
thank God for it - Brothers I dont wish to
Deceive you or any other Person. I take
it Very hard with been Detained here in
a Place Like this - to Up hold and
Incurage this Unlawful afair - its time
this afair was desided in a Court - its my
money they are Spending and Dividing
and Disposing of my Property and Shares —

Jan 14. 1900. Ratains his old delusion
a fantastic manner about the

James Rhodes

Number of admission: 1846
Admitted: 25 July 1893.
Age: Fifty.
Religious persuasion: Protestant.
Married, single or widowed: Single.
Occupation: Painter.
Previous place of abode: Woking Prison.
Name and residence of nearest known relative: Joseph Rhodes (brother), 1 Bath Street, Leeds.
Asylum: Has been in Broadmoor Asylum for the criminally insane.

Epileptic: Not.
Suicidal: Not.
Dangerous to others: Not.
Diagnosis: Mania.

Facts observed by D. Nicholson, Medical Supt Broadmoor: Chronic Mania with delusions that he is of immense wealth, of which attempts are being made to remove from him, that several of his relatives have visited the Asylum and been brutally ill-treated by the others.

Other facts communicated: That he is injured and being drugged and poisoned.

Mental state: That he was sent to Broadmoor to be swindled but that the doctor and minister would not allow such to be done. Says that it was not a single person that was trying to drug him but that it was a company. He had a doctor's injection to say that he was a sane man but he gave it to a friend from whom he can get it back at any time, his memory is defective, he says that he was forty years in Broadmoor, whereas he was ten, that his people are about these grounds somewhere to see that he is not robbed, that he has great estates, the buildings on which date back to the fifteenth century.

James Rhodes was a direct transfer from Broadmoor Asylum for the criminally insane. Prior to being admitted to Broadmoor, James had been in Woking Prison serving a ten-year sentence for burglary. From the moment James entered Menston Asylum, he maintained his delusions of grandeur, thinking that large sums of money were due to him. He felt that he was being kept at Menston to deprive him of his immense wealth, and in January 1898 made good his escape while exercising from the airing court. He got as far as Leeds, no doubt hoping to protect his apparent wealth, however he was recaptured within a day. On 21 April 1896, it was noted, 'Patient is taken up with his ideas and delusions and often writes long letters and statements about his imagined property.' One of his letters can be seen on the opposite page. Despite his desire to be free, James was to spend twenty-nine years at Menston before dying in 1922, aged seventy-nine.

He was buried in Buckle Lane Cemetery on 2 October 1922, row 29, grave 27.

'She is resistive when interfered with and smacked
the night nurse in the face'

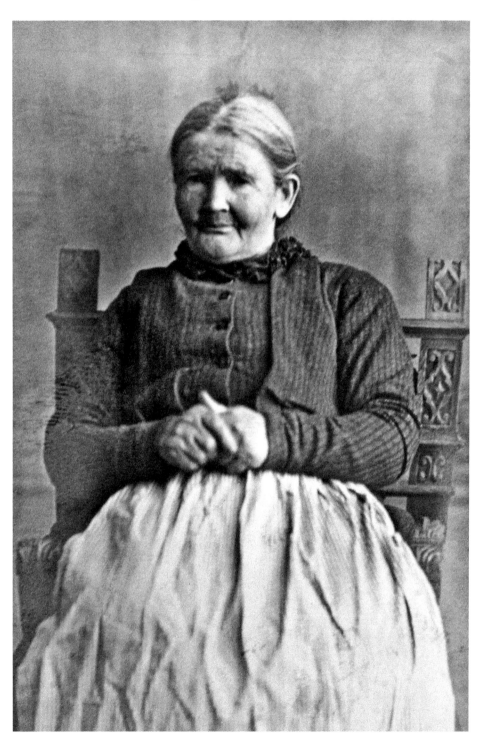

Hannah Wood

Number of admission: 7586

Admitted: 11 January 1907.

Age: Sixty-two.

Age on first attack: Not known.

Religious persuasion: Roman Catholic.

Married, single or widowed: Widowed.

Occupation: Housework.

Previous place of abode: Leeds Union Workhouse Infirmary.

Nearest known relative: William Holleran (Son), 13 Portland Terrace, Leeds.

Relatives similarly affected: Not known.

Relieving officer: George Farrar.

Whether first attack: Not known.

Insane: Few days.

Supposed cause: Not known.

Dangerous to others: Yes.

Facts observed by James Allan: She has delusions that her brother Thomas McGuiness wants to supplant her in the Catholic throne of Ireland. Also that she thinks that the attendant here is a Fenian and a poisoner and that her food here has been poisoned.

Other facts communicated: Hannah Roberts from Leeds Union Infirmary says that Hannah Wood refused her breakfast this morning and threw the dishes at the attendant. She gets very noisy and excitable, also imagines that this is the place where Queens are beheaded.

Mental state: She is very excited and noisy. She suffers from hallucinations and also from delusions and is also very exalted. She is restless and will not stay in bed at night. She is resistive when interfered with and smacked the night nurse in the face. She sings and gesticulates constantly.

What Irish-born Hannah's medical records do not state is the important fact that she had recently lost her husband, Thomas. He was clearly on her mind, because it was noted in January 1910 that she continually repeats the story of him and his part in the Indian Mutiny. Throughout her time as a patient at Menston, Hannah did very little work. She did, however, retain her delusions and good health, although by early 1915 she had developed cardiac trouble.

Hannah passed away on 30 March 1917 at 3.07 p.m. of valvular heart disease, which was confirmed by a post-mortem performed by Dr Richard Kirwan. She was seventy-two.

Hannah was buried Buckle Lane Cemetery on 4 April 1917, row 13, grave 20, after nine years at Menston Asylum.

'Delusions of wealth and they are inclined to be violent'

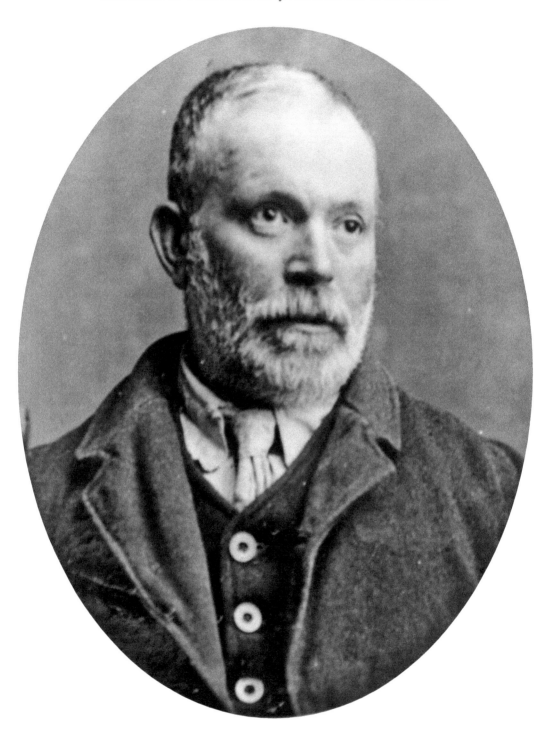

James Green

Number of admission: 7652
Admitted: 19 March 1907.
Age: Fifty-three.
Age on first attack: Not known.
Occupation: Brewery cooper.
Religious persuasion: Church of England.
Married, single or widowed: Married.
Chargeable to: Hawley.
Previous place of abode: 13 South Field Place/Union Workhouse Infirmary Leeds.
Asylum: Has not been in any asylums.
Name and residence of nearest known relative: Mary Ann Green, 13 South Field Place, Armley, Leeds.
Relieving Officer: T. Allan/Police Superintendent.

Facts observed by E. H. Howell: Facial tremors, irregular pupils, dirty in habit, untidy and destructive of clothing, delusions of wealth and they are inclined to be violent.

Other facts communicated by Walter J. Ford, HM Prison, Hull: Tremulous, dirty, destructive, violent at times (struck various officers), delusions at night: to throw a man over his head, of wealth, to buy a motor car and tour the world.

Supposed cause: Not known.
Suicidal: Not known.
Dangerous to others: Not known.

Apparent cause of death: Degeneration of the heart.
Whether or not ascertained by Post-Mortem examination: Yes.
Time and date of death: 5.30 p.m., 10 September 1907.
Duration of disease of which patient died: Long.
Name of persons present at death: W. Barnsley.

Researching the life of James, who was born in Hull, it appears that he spent a lot of his later life either in prison or the workhouse. When James was admitted to Menston Asylum directly from Hull Prison, it was quite literally the end of the line for him. During his short spell as a patient, James became convinced he would be blown up with gas, and that his clothes would be stolen if he took them off. Within six months of his initial reception, James had passed away. Sadly, as with all the other people in Buckle Lane Cemetery, no one came to collect his remains.

He was buried at Buckle Lane Cemetery on 5 July 1907, row 11, grave 7.

'If pressed with questions the only answer she gives is "I don't know"'

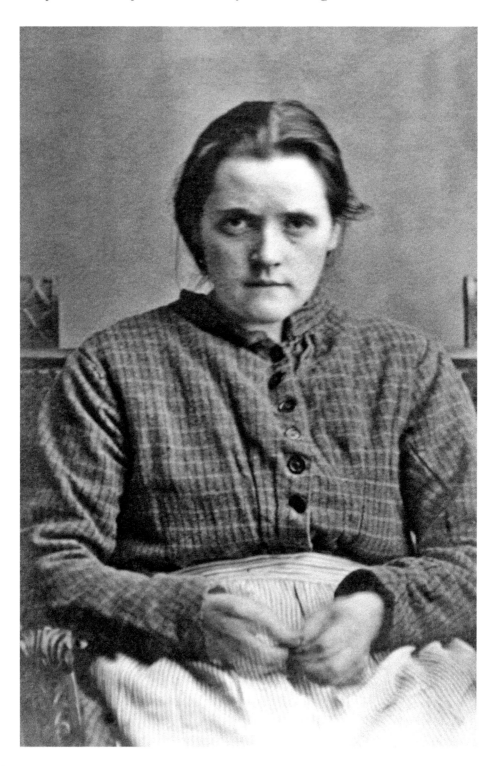

Elizabeth Davies

Number of admission: 8363

Admitted: 4 May 1909.

Age: Twenty-four.

Age on first attack: Twenty-one.

Religious persuasion: Baptist.

Occupation: Drawer.

Married, single or widowed: Single.

Chargeable to: Keighley Union Workhouse.

Previous place of abode: South View, Cullingworth.

Name of nearest known relative: Father, John Davies, South View, Cullingworth, Bradford.

Relatives similarly affected: A cousin to her mother.

Relieving officer: J. H. Crossley.

Asylum: Has been in Menston Asylum.

Attack: Second.

Insane: Six months.

Supposed cause: Not known.

Dangerous to others: Yes.

Facts observed by Thomas Taylor: Incoherent is her conversation, uses abominable language and her actions and behaviour are quite contrary to her usual conduct.

Other facts communicated: Her mother tells me that she has become quite unmanageable, uses vile language and goes into the adjoining school yard and without provocation hits the children and uses foul names to the teachers.

Mental state: When patient is spoken to she answers irrationally. Her conversation is incoherent. If pressed with questions the only answer she gives is, 'I don't know'. She takes no interest whatever in her surroundings, does not know where she is, and is usually silent and self-absorbed. She becomes excited at times and is then violent and dangerous. She is apparently deluded, though she will not speak of her delusions.

Elizabeth, born in Whitworth, Lancashire, moved to Cullingworth, West Yorkshire, with her parents, John and Eliza, in the late 1880s. It is apparent from her records that she had previously been admitted to Menston and been discharged, either recovered or relieved. Sadly, when she arrived back in 1909, aged twenty-four, she was never to leave, spending some forty years at the hospital, before dying in 1948, the very year the institution was taken over by the newly formed NHS. Throughout her time as a patient she was consistently reduced in her mental capacity and unable to work, apart from a short spell in the laundry loading the clothes horse.

Elizabeth was laid to rest at Buckle Lane Cemetery on 28 August 1948, aged sixty-four. Her funeral was paid for by E. M. Horner, West Riding Health Authority, the first time such a payment had been made for any funeral at the cemetery.

'States that he has lately been visited by Prince Consort'

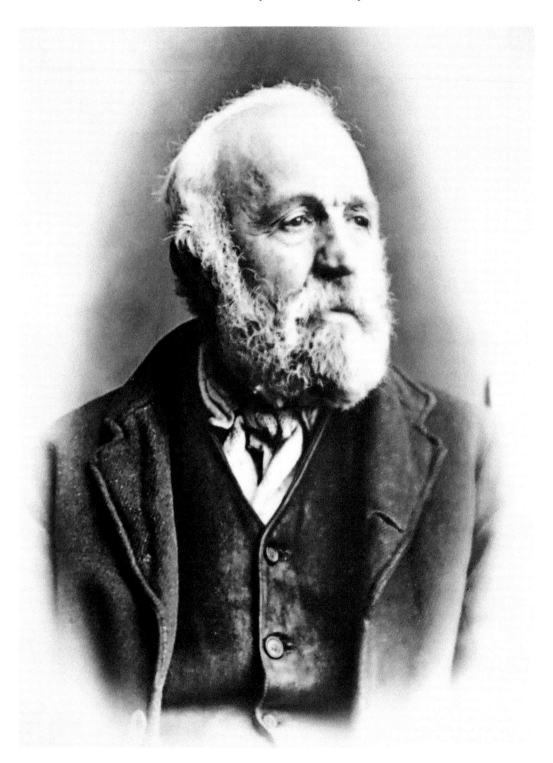

George Gregg

Number of admission: 327
Admitted: 10 May 1889.
Age: Sixty-three.
Religious persuasion: None.
Married, single or widowed: Single.
Previous place of abode: Ripon.
Occupation: Skinner.
Chargeable to: Ripon.
Name and residence of nearest known relative: John Gregg, Ripon.

Facts observed by T. I. Frankland M.R.C.S., Ripon, 28 January 1857: His extremely violent and irrational behaviour. His declaration of being a person of independent property and his refusal to maintain himself in consequence. Transfer from North Riding Asylum.

Other facts communicated: His violent and irrational language to his friends.

History: A transfer from the North Riding Asylum, to which he was removed from Dunnington House near York in 1859, having been admitted into the latter asylum upon a certificate dated 28 January 1857.

Mental state: Patient is moody and preoccupied – irrational and somewhat incoherent – says he hears voices but cannot give any definite account of his hallucinations and would appear to be very affected by them. States that he has lately been visited by Prince Consort. His memory is fair but he is decidedly demented.

Attack: First attack.
Diagnosis: Chronic mania.
Causation: Not ascertained.
Prognosis: Unfavourable.
Treatment: Palliative.

George was the eldest of seven children born to John and Ann Gregg of Ripon. His father was, until his death in 1882, the Town Crier for the town. George appears to have led a normal life up until January 1855, when he was given eighteen months imprisonment for larceny (theft). It is not known if his time in prison brought about his delusions of being related to the Prince of Wales, but by late January 1857, he was a patient at the former York Asylum (now known as Bootham Park). It was noted in 1895, 'Patient is a quiet, fairly useful and tidy man. Employs himself fairly usefully on the farm.' George was at times stubborn but generally regarded by staff to be quiet and manageable, while still retaining delusions of royal descent.

He died on 20 September 1900, with the apparent cause of death being malignant disease of liver. George was buried at Buckle Lane Cemetery on 25 September 1900, row 27, grave 30, aged seventy-four.

'Talks foolishly and frequently about her husband as if he were alive'

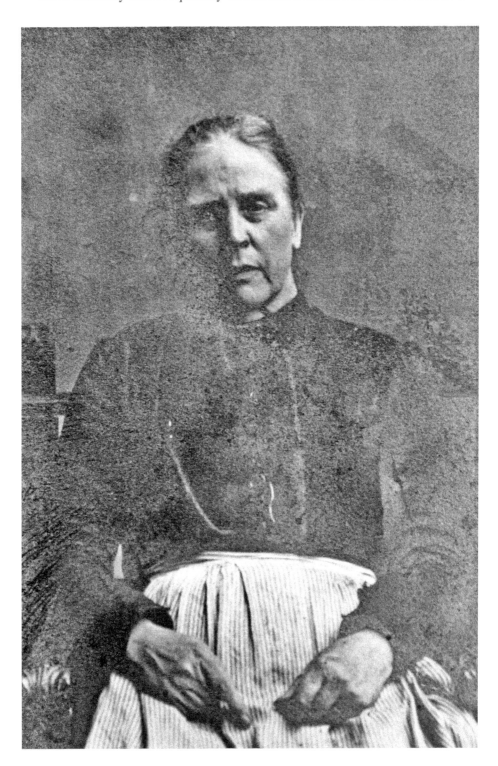

Mary Ann Strickland

Number of admission: 7462

Admitted: 7 September 1906.

Age: Fifty-three.

Age on first attack: Fifty-three.

Married, single or widowed: Widow.

Occupation: Housewife.

Religious persuasion: Church of England.

Relieving Officer: George Farrar.

Previous place of abode: 22 Jubilee Street, Leeds.

Nearest known relative: Sarah Fozzard (sister), 9 Ethan Terrace, Leeds.

Attack: First.

Insane: Six months.

Supposed cause: Alcohol and death of husband.

Facts observed by J. Swing: Interest in household affairs almost nil, is daily expecting her husband home from hospital (he has been dead for fifteen months), memory distinctly impaired (History of heavy drinking for years).

Other facts communicated: Mrs Sarah Fozzard (sister), Leeds, says her sister is suffering from loss of memory, talks foolishly and frequently about her husband as if he were alive, though he died fifteen months ago. Will not prepare any meals or wash herself.

Mental state: Patient says she has been in the asylum sometime and that her husband (who is dead) brought her here yesterday but was unable to stop. She shows little memory for past events, though she answers coherently. She wanders about the ward at times in a half dazed condition.

Mary never got over the death of her husband John, a surgical mechanician. For many years, she believed him to be still alive and was forever looking for him. When spoken to she would get emotional and weep continuously. As the years rolled by, her memory of her past life diminished and she busied herself with cleaning the ward and a little sewing. Once a wealthy woman when her husband was alive, Mary lived out her thirty-two years at Menston as a pauper inmate before dying in 1938.

She was buried at Buckle Lane Cemetery on 30 November 1938, row 22, grave 4.

'A disposition for blood having killed a sheep and drunk the blood'

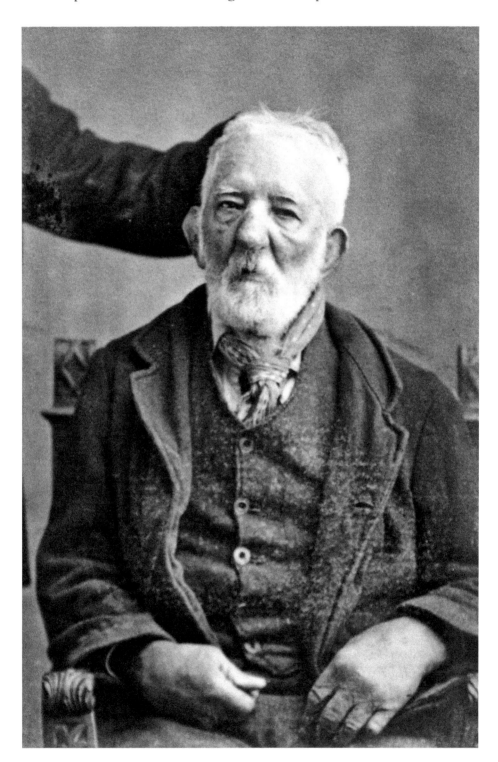

John Longthorn

Number of admission: 113

Admitted: 17 November 1888.

Age: Seventy.

Age on first attack: Twenty-four.

Married, single or widowed: Single.

Religious persuasion: Not known.

Occupation: Labourer.

Previous place of abode: Skipton.

Nearest known relative: Joseph Longthorn, 8 Rook Street, Nelson, Lancashire.

Relatives similarly affected: Relatives not known.

Relieving officer: Simon Hunter.

Whether first attack: First attack.

Insane: Two weeks.

Supposed cause: Dementia.

Facts observed by William Mansden: He is depressed in spirits, as on admission, and of a monotonous disposition, if asked any questions he walks away without answering. Bodily health is good.

Other facts communicated: Can read, relatives not known, the first attack, depression of spirits, a disposition for blood, having killed a sheep and drunk the blood. He is not mischievous.

History: Patient is a transfer from Wakefield Asylum, into which he was admitted upon a certificate dated June 11, 1853.

Mental state: He has a quiet, melancholy, demented appearance. He whispers and appears to be afraid of his own voice.

John was one of the first male patients to be admitted to the new Menston Asylum. No stranger to asylum life, he had spent the previous thirty-five years at Wakefield Asylum, being admitted in the summer of 1853, aged thirty-five, for depression. Sadly, John was to spend sixty-one years under care and treatment before he died in 1914, aged ninety-six. The picture of John you see opposite was taken just three years before his death when, even in his nineties, he still took pride in his appearance and attempted to clean the ward.

It was noted in August 1903: 'Since last note this old man has completed his fiftieth year of residence under care and treatment. He shows no change mentally.'

John died of senile decay on 28 March 1914. The cause of death was ascertained by post-mortem.

The oldest resident in the cemetery is Emma Stead, aged ninety-seven; John, at ninety-six, is the second oldest resident buried at Buckle Lane.

John was buried on 2 April 1914, row 29, grave 14, after sixty-one years under care and treatment.

'Patient tripped on her dress today and fell,
fracturing both tibia and fibula'

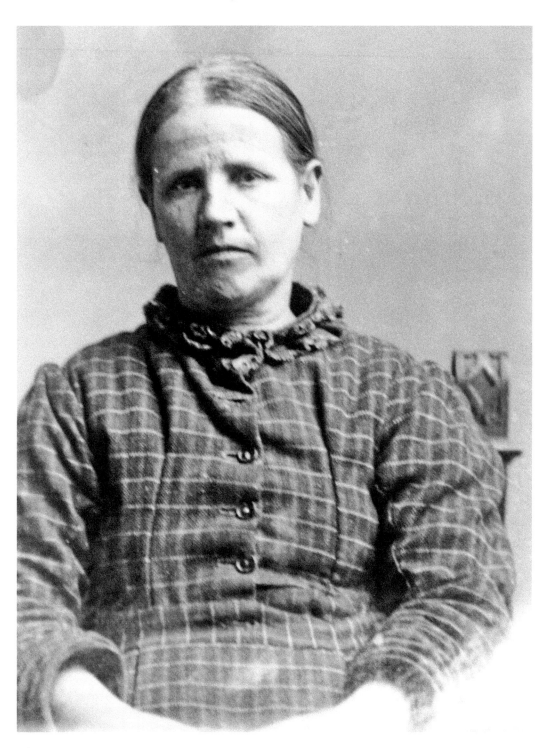

Mary Kemmey

Number of admission: 4361
Admitted: 24 September 1898.
Age: Forty-six.
Religious persuasion: Church of England.
Married, single or widowed: Single.
Occupation: Mill hand.
Asylum: Has not been in any asylum.
Previous place of abode: Leeds Union Workhouse Infirmary.
Name of nearest known relative: Emily Kemmey (sister), 28 Laskey Street, Leeds.
Relieving Officer: G. Farrar.

Attack: First.
Supposed cause: Not known.

Facts observed by J. Allan: She has delusions that the residence of her house has been stolen and that her money has been taken from the PO Savings Bank. She is morbidly suspicious, thinks her doctor has experimented on her throat with a view to benefit a neighbour suffering from a sore throat.

Other facts communicated: She does very little work as she thinks it is no use to save money and get robbed of it, says that a lady named Miss Ford has gained by her friendship while Mr Stead has lost much by the want of it and says that all, including the police, are against her.

Mental state: She exhibits a good deal of general restlessness and mental confusion, shifts about and plucks her clothing. She answers questions readily but mostly incoherently. Her memory is much impaired and very little information can be extracted from her. She is full of delusions and states that during the last few years the neighbours have been continually robbing her and that sixty dresses, dozens of pairs of boots and even bedsteads have been stolen from her house without her knowing at the time. She declares also that they have managed to get all her money out of the savings bank.

Mary came from a large family of Irish descent and for most of her life lived with her sisters Margaret and Jane in All Saints, East Leeds. The sisters all worked in the linen mill, Mary herself was employed as a linen yarn winder. Very quickly after entering Menston, she began to improve and was free of excitement, though still retaining some delusions. On 30 November 1898 she tripped over her dress and broke her tibia on her left leg, which apparently healed very well, as it was noted on 1 February 1899: 'She is able to walk a little about the ward. She is quiet, pleasant and good tempered and free from excitement.' Mary continued to be pleasant and good tempered until 1905 when it was claimed she had become suspicious and somewhat resistive and abusive. Sadly, on 24 April 1908 Mary passed away at 3.45 p.m., in the presence of nurse Keena. The post-mortem ascertained the cause of death as a malignant disease of the breast and liver.

She was buried at Buckle Lane Cemetery on 30 April 1908, row 14, grave 11, aged 56.

'Has a delusion that he is coming in for thousands when he is twenty-one'

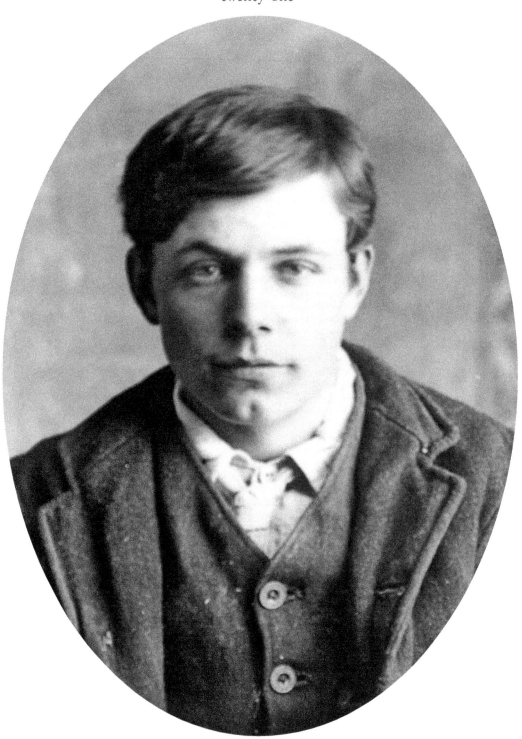

Joseph Smithies

Number of admission: 7778

Admitted: 16 July 1907.

Age: Eighteen.

Religious persuasion: Church of England.

Occupation: Assistant Cabinet Maker.

Chargeable to: Private.

Previous place of abode: 26 Ripon Road.

Name of nearest known relative: Mrs Sarah Ann Smithies, 26 Ripon Road, Harrogate.

Relatives similarly affected: Father, Samuel Smithies.

Insane: Two weeks.

Facts observed by A. W. H. Walker: He is surly, does not readily answer any questions, asked why he left his lodgings, reply is simply because he did not wish to stay though he admits they were comfortable, says he will not work.

Other facts communicated: The mother, Mrs Sarah Smithies of 26 Ripon Road, Harrogate, says that she has been many times in terror of her life at the hands her son, Joseph Smithies. His age, eighteen years, precludes her from having any physical control over him. He is subject to ungovernable attacks of temper in which she says he throws things at his mother or sisters. His language is vile on such occasions and he frequently defies all in the house. Mr Charles England, 36 Ripon Road, Harrogate, says he has frequently met with Joseph Smithies during the past year and was called in the night before last, says he has heard him several times threaten to go for the mother.

Patient has a bad family history. His father is in York Asylum. He has been in gaol twice, he is excited and restless. Has delusions of persecution, thinks that his mother has ill-treated him, that it is through her that he was put in prison and that he was sent here. He is emotional and has occasional fits of passion. Has little or no self-control and will not settle to employment for any length of time. Has a delusion that he is coming in for thousands when he is twenty-one.

August 1 1907: Is not so deluded, now understands that his mother has done the best she could for him.
December 1 1907: He has improved mentally and has been working well.
December 31 1907: Finally discharged today.

Admitted as a private patient, Joseph's family paid 20s a week for his upkeep. We can see from the record he was in fact discharged as improved in December 1907; however, he was to return to Menston Asylum, but this time as a pauper patient. Joseph was possibly not quite as deluded as the notes make out, for he was the grandson of wealthy Joseph Smithies, who owned Perseverance Mills in Elland. Joseph Snr, in 1861, employed 100 hands and could well have had a trust in place for the young Joseph.

It is not known when Joseph the younger returned to Menston Asylum. However, upon his death in 1942, aged fifty-three, none of his four siblings collected his remains. He was buried at Buckle Lane Cemetery, 17 January 1942, row 11, grave 3.

'She says her employer was a violent man and gave her a great fright'

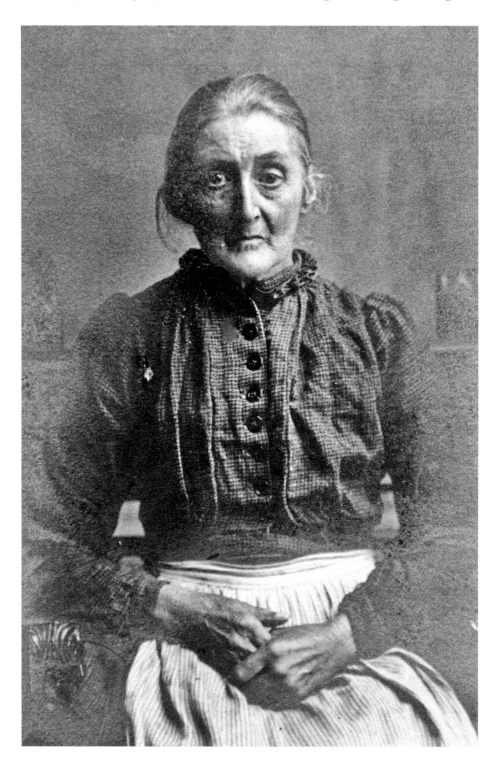

Elizabeth Walker

Admitted: 29 January 1907.

Age: Sixty-two.

Age on first attack: Fifty.

Religious persuasion: Church of England.

Married, single or widowed: Widow.

Occupation: Domestic Servant.

Chargeable to: Wharfedale.

Previous place of abode: 19 Lombard Street, Rawdon.

Asylum: Wakefield and Menston previously.

Name of nearest known relative: Brother, Mr Arthur Teale, 9 Bedley Grove, Leeds.

Relieving Officer: John Greenwood.

Attack: Not the first.

Insane: Several weeks.

Suicidal: Yes.

Dangerous to others: Not.

Facts observed by C. H. Dickens: The patient's appearance of melancholia. She asserts she has no control of herself and subject to sudden impulses. Has been in an asylum before for attempted suicide. Has had dreams.

Other facts communicated by Mrs Hindle, her niece, 19 Lombard Street: The last week she had been very depressed, doesn't talk and says she has no control of herself and is afraid of what she might do and has been put into an asylum twice before for some time.

Mental state: She is very miserable and depressed and apparently frightened and apprehensive. Says she is afraid of those around her and sits biting her nails, looking furtively at her surroundings. She says her employer was a violent man and gave her a great fright.

Elizabeth was no stranger to asylum life when she entered Menston Asylum in 1907. Previously, she had been admitted and discharged at both Wakefield and Menston Asylums; however, on this occasion she was to see out her days in Menston. For the first four years, she was consistently depressed, gloomy, silent and in poor health, rendering her being moved to ward 15, the female sick and infirm block. On 15 July 1911, she had improved vastly and it was noted: 'Is much brighter and appears to have got rid of her suicidal tendencies. She has a great antipathy to another patient, Hannah Sugden, who makes her feel weak and queer. She says she suffers a great deal from her nerves and that before she came here, her employer said he would make her die a quick death and this badly affects her. In fair bodily health, eats and sleeps well.' This was short-lived, because in April 1912 she began to lose weight and suffered a good deal of abdominal pain. In spite of the remedies applied, Elizabeth died on 24 May 1914 at 7.10 p.m., in the presence of nurse Summerscale. The apparent cause of death was colitis.

Elizabeth was buried at Buckle Lane Cemetery on 29 May 1912, row 24, grave 5, aged sixty-seven.

'Says that the stationmaster at York talks to him here and tells him he is soon to go home'

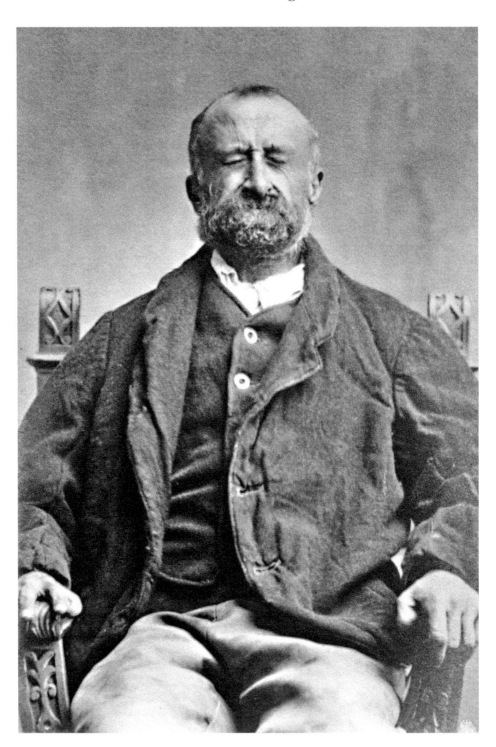

Frederick William Smithson

Number of admission: 2223

Admitted: 29 September 1894.

Age: Thirty-one.

Age on first attack: Twenty-five?

Religious persuasion: Church of England.

Married, single or widowed: Single.

Occupation: Architect.

Chargeable to: Leeds.

Previous place of abode: Leeds Union Workhouse Infirmary.

Relieving Officer: J. Radcliffe.

Asylum: Has been in The Retreat, York.

Insane: Six and a half years.

Supposed cause: Unknown.

Epileptic: Yes.

Suicidal: Yes.

Dangerous to others: Yes.

Facts observed by J. Allan, Leeds: When pressed with questions, he occasionally answers but all the time talking quickly and earnestly says he is talking to Armstrong, an architect. When asked to write down what Armstrong says to him, he writes letters and some words correctly, but not so as to form an intelligible sentence, he also says that the stationmaster at York talks to him here and tells him he is soon to go home.

Other facts communicated by J. Newell: Says that he is always talking to himself and never to any of the other inmates, that he puts soap in his mouth and bites it.

9 April 1895: No fits since admission, is very destructive, does no work, eats and sleeps well. In fair bodily health.

6 May 1895: Is very untidy and destructive, is not employable at all, in fair bodily health.

20 Oct 1899: In silent element, he becomes at times noisy and excited, he keeps his eyes fixed on the ground and seems very depressed, very weak.

Frederick, the son of George and Lucy Smithson, was in 1891 an apprentice chemist-druggist, although by 1894 his profession was noted to be that of an architect. Very little information is available regarding the circumstances that brought about his breakdown, however we do know he spent twenty years at Menston in a mindless condition, and died just months before the hostilities commenced in 1914.

Frederick was buried at Buckle Lane Cemetery on 9 March 1914, row 29, grave 10.

'She states that she saw the late King Edward when he came
to Thornton'

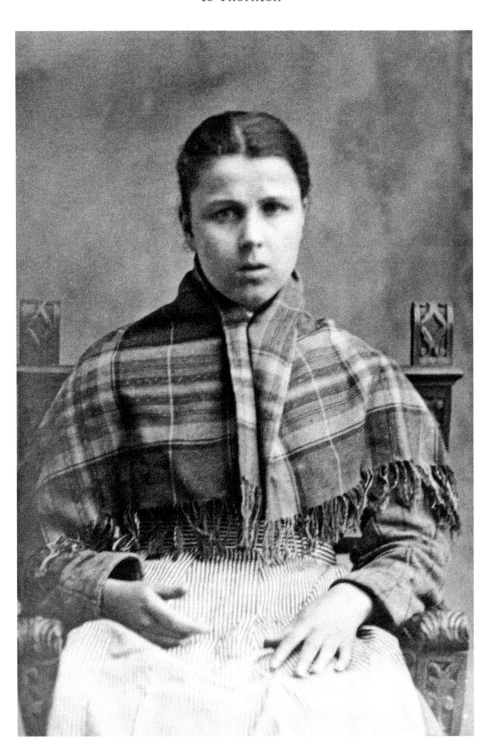

Mary Holmes

Number of admission: 9080
Admitted: 21 March 1911.
Age: Seventeen.
Age on first attack: Fourteen.
Religious persuasion: Wesleyan.
Married, single or widowed: Single.
Occupation: Worsted Spinner.
Chargeable to: N. Bierley.
Asylum: Has not been in any asylum.
Previous place of abode: Bradford Union Workhouse.
Name of nearest known relative: Robert Holmes (father), 6 Mount Pleasant, Bradford.
Relatives similarly affected: Not.
Relieving Officer: G. H. Margison.

Attacks: Not first.
Insane: Some years.
Supposed cause: Not known.
Epileptic: Yes.
Suicidal: Not.
Dangerous to others: Not.

Observations: Patient is sullen and irritable in her manner and will not engage in any conversation. She resents any interference and is resistant to examination and tends to become violent. She shows no interest in her surroundings and does not recognise where she is.

Facts observed by W. Cuncliffe: She suffers from attacks of epilepsy after which she is very excitable, shouting and singing and will not stay in bed but throws herself about on the floor. She states that she saw the late King Edward when he came to Thornton, which is not true.

Other facts communicated by Annie L. Connor, Union Workhouse, Bradford: States that Holmes is at times very troublesome, shouting and singing for hours at a time and being unable to keep still. After her fits she is quite lost, running away from the premises not knowing where she is going.

Mary was the daughter of Robert (a bricklayer) and Hannah Holmes of Thornton, Bradford, she was the second youngest of four children. Mary was sent to Menston directly from Clayton Workhouse Infirmary, located about two miles away from her home. Sadly, at just seventeen years old, she was destined to spend the rest of her short life at Menston, dying there in December 1818, aged just twenty-four. Throughout her time at Menston, she never showed any sign of improvement, being in the main restless and incapable of any rational conversation.

Mary was laid to rest at Buckle Lane Cemetery on 20 December 1918, row 21, grave 34.

'He is a disciple of the Lord, that he is cousin to Jack the Ripper'

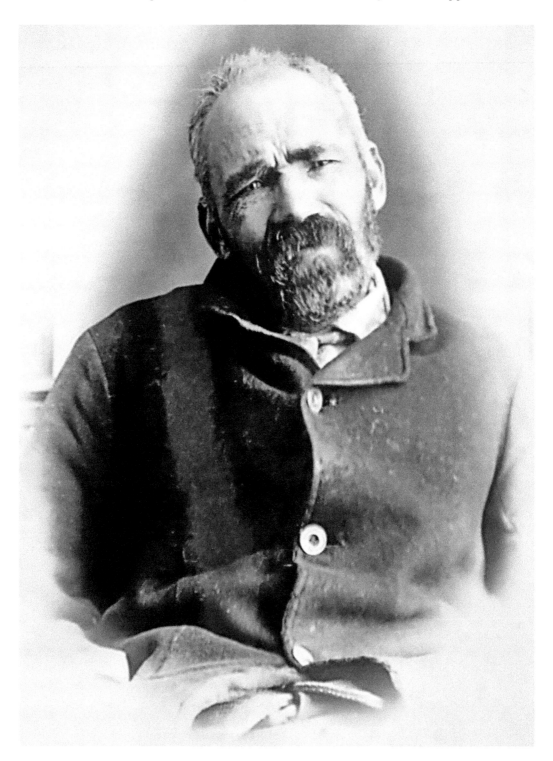

Michael King

Number of admission: 481

Admitted: 24 September 1889.

Age: Forty-three.

Age on first attack: Forty-three.

Religious persuasion: Roman Catholic.

Married, single or widowed: Single.

Occupation: Labourer.

Chargeable to: Bradford.

Previous place of abode: Bradford Union Workhouse Infirmary.

Name and residence of nearest known relative: Patrick Cumming (friend), 48 Wellington Street, Bradford.

Dangerous to others: Yes.

Facts observed by W. B. Proctor F.R.C.S. Bradford Infirmary: He is quite insane and maniacal. Raves and shouts and gesticulates, is full of delusions about himself and religion. That he can, that they can come to him and that he is a disciple of the Lord, that he is cousin to Jack the Ripper.

Other facts communicated: The nurse reports that he is restless, excited and violent, has to be strictly watched or would escape. Is full of delusions about himself, that he has supreme power on the devil, that he saves sinners and that he is first cousin of Jack the Ripper.

History: Patient has been betting on horses and worried himself. Has been a moderate drinker. Very little information obtained, stated to have been threatened and frightened.

Mental state: Patient is surly and uncommunicative – garrulous and irrational. Will not reply to questions, meeting them with silence or with others. Asked where he is, says 'you know as well as I do', but does not appear to appreciate his position and surroundings. Says that during the last few days he has been touched in his brain ... Neither admits or denies the statements in the certificates and exhibits so much confusion and distrust that nothing whatever can be made out of him.

Michael, who was born in Claremorris, Co. Mayo, was a good outside worker and always talking about going home, but was doubtful whether he could ever live outside the asylum. The medical staff deemed him fit for discharge on 4 December 1890, however he returned on 13 December of his own free will, convinced he had been followed in the street and everyone was against him.

In 1894, he escaped and got as far as Leeds before he was arrested and sent back to the asylum, where his previous freedom was removed and he was kept on the ward. Michael was to spend eleven years in total at Menston, before dying on 21 April 1900, aged fifty-four, from necrosis of the tibia. His escape to Leeds is detailed on the following pages.

He was buried at Buckle Lane Cemetery, 24 April 1900, row 26, grave 36.

A VISITOR FROM MENSTON.—A robust-looking fellow, about forty years of age, named Michael King, appeared in the dock at the Leeds Police-court yesterday, charged with wandering abroad whilst of unsound mind. About 9.10 on Monday night, the prisoner went up to Police-constable Ive, in Boar-lane, and asked him to find him lodgings. Asked where he had come from, he replied, " From Menston," whereupon the policeman removed him to the Town Hall.—The Mayor: It was not merely because the man said he was from Menston that you locked him up?—Police-constable Ive: No, sir; he talked very queer.—Superintendent McWilliam: He has the uniform of the Menston Asylum upon him.—Prisoner: I left the asylum at half-past four on a visit, but when I got to this town there were so many people about, and it was so wet, that I asked that gentleman (the constable) to accommodate me with lodgings.—The Mayor: You have no objections to going back to Menston, I suppose?—Prisoner: No, I have no objection, except the little one that they haven't given me sufficient medical care. They haven't looked after my chest as they ought to do. —The Mayor: You will be given into the care of the officer from Menston.

A VISITOR FROM MENSTON – A robust-looking fellow, about forty years of age, named Michael King, appeared in the dock at the Leeds Police-court yesterday, charged with wandering abroad whilst of unsound mind. About 9.10 on Monday night, the prisoner went up to Police-constable Ive, in Boar-lane, and asked him to find him lodgings. Asked where he had come from, he replied 'From Menston,' whereupon the policeman removed him to the Town Hall. – The Mayor: It was not merely because the man said he was from Menston, that you locked him up? Police-constable Ive: No, sir, he talked very queer – Superintendent McWilliam: He has the uniform of the Menston Asylum upon him – Prisoner: I left the asylum at half-past four on a visit, but when I got to this town there were so many people about, and it was so wet, that I asked that gentleman (the constable) to accommodate me with lodgings – The Mayor: You have no objections to going back to Menston, I suppose? – Prisoner: No, I have no objection, except the little one that they haven't given me sufficient medical care. They haven't looked after my chest as they ought to do – The Mayor: You will be given into the care of the officer from Menston.

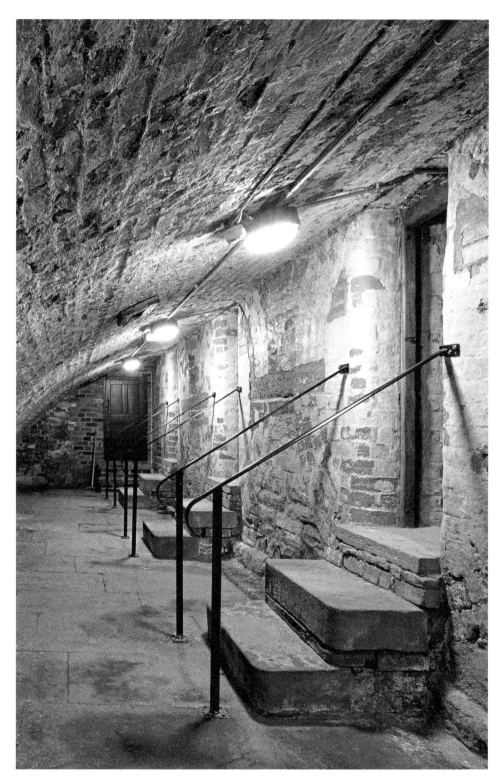

The Victorian cells below Leeds Town Hall.

'She is constantly striking and throwing things at other patients'

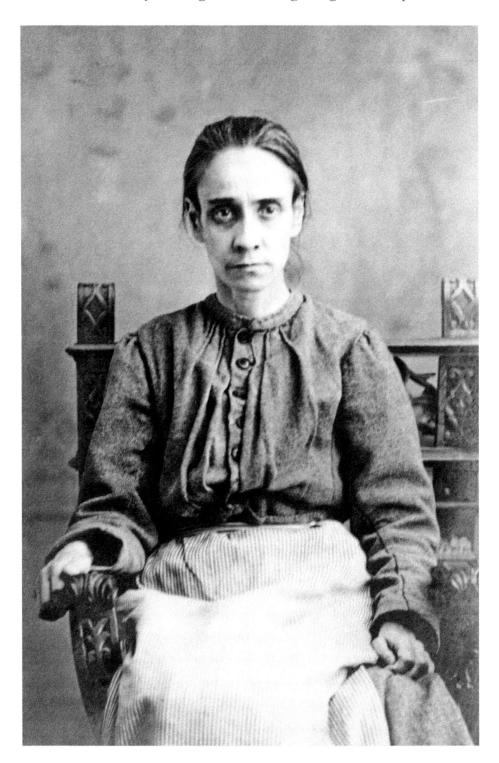

Catherine Kennedy

Number of admission: 9170
Admitted: 8 June 1911.
Age: Thirty-eight.
Age on first attack: Infancy.
Married, single or widowed: Single.
Occupation: Nil.
Previous place of abode: Bradford Union Workhouse Infirmary.
Nearest known relative: Mary Kennedy (mother), Daisy Lane, Daisy Hill, Bradford.
Relatives similarly affected: Not known.
Relieving officer: Alfred Wood.

First attack: Not known.
Insane: Since 1907.
Supposed cause: Congenital.
Epilepsy: Yes.
Suicidal: Not.
Dangerous to others: Yes.

Facts observed by B. H. Slater: She glares and frowns and gesticulates wildly, banging her hands on the window sill against the door and apparently threatens violence. She violently bangs the door. She rummages amongst drawers as though looking for something.

Other facts communicated by workhouse: She is constantly striking and throwing things at other patients, often refuses her food and throws it at those who bring it. She is subject to epileptic fits.

Physical condition: Dark and sparely nourished, tongue clean, circulatory system and pulse feeble. Knee jerks present. Pupils are equal and active.

Mental state: Patient is deaf and dumb. She lies in bed burying her head under the clothes and will not be interfered with. She takes her food and is quiet.

Catherine, born in Sligo, Ireland, was deaf and dumb from birth. Her mother, Mary, although living in Bradford, was staying with her nephew, Richard O'Keefe, at 14 Daisy Hill, and had been doing since at least 1901; however, there is no record of Catherine being with her. Given the amount of management required to care for Catherine from birth, it is likely she spent much of her later life in either the workhouse infirmary or some form of institutional care elsewhere. The only improvement of Catherine's during her time at Menston was her general health, and the considered opinion of the medical staff that she was no longer a danger. After spending thirty-six years at Menston, Catherine passed away in 1947.

She was buried at Buckle Lane Cemetery on 11 March 1947, row 2, grave 29.

'He calls God "Billy Pudding". He has frequent conversations with "Billy"'

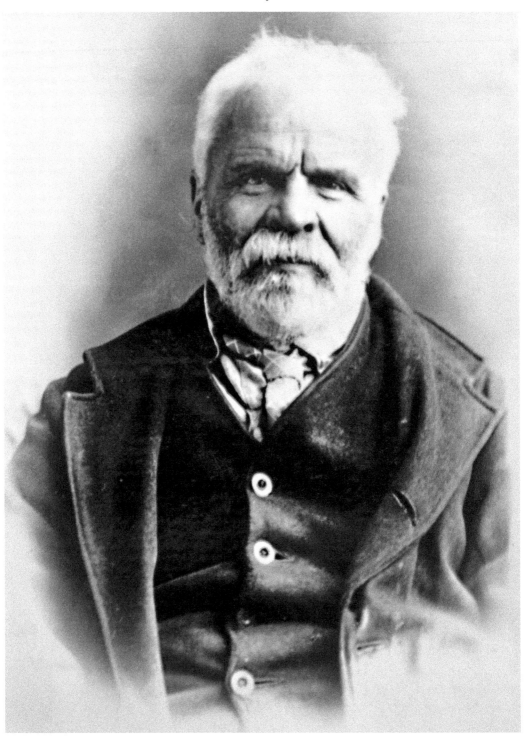

John Wright

Number of admission: 76

Admitted: 7 November 1888.

Age: Forty-seven.

Age on first attack: Forty-three.

Religious persuasion: Church of England.

Married, single or widowed: Single.

Occupation: Saddle tree maker.

Chargeable to: Ripon.

Previous place of abode: Ripon.

Name and residence of nearest known relative: Winston Wright (brother), Barefoot Lane, Ripon.

Relieving officer: Henry Williams.

Supposed cause: Not known.

Suicidal: Yes.

Facts observed by W. Dixon Jefferson, Ripon: Vacant and wandering, always suffering from melancholia, he states that nobody wants him to live and that he will do away with himself when he has the chance.

Other facts communicated by the sister, Ann: He is constantly attempting to do away with himself, he has attempted to kill his brothers with a knife, he is always trying to evade them. Very cunning and always suffering from melancholia.

History: Patient is a transfer from Wadsley Asylum, into which he was admitted 23 July 1884. From Wadsley, he is reported as somewhat dangerous and unreliable, he has a delusion that he is God.

Mental state: Patient is very deluded, says he is the son of God, has received a spirit from heaven, says he was sent by 'the overpowering laws of nature', that India, America and Australia were represented there and falls suddenly in a semi-coherent grandiose state, he is thoroughly possessed by his delusions.

2 Dec 1891: Patient has delusions, he calls God 'Billy Pudding'. He has frequent conversations with 'Billy' and tells him many things which govern his daily life. Bodily condition very good.

Despite being incarcerated in the asylum, John was quite happy conversing with 'Billy Pudding', whose advice totally governed John's daily life. Described as deluded and grandiose, John was also bright, happy and a good worker. Voicing his delusions continually ensured that he lived out his days at Menston. John died in March 1913, aged seventy-three.

He was buried at Buckle Lane Cemetery on 27 March 1913, row 26, grave 13.

'Says she wants to go home and says her mother is not her mother and she is not at home'

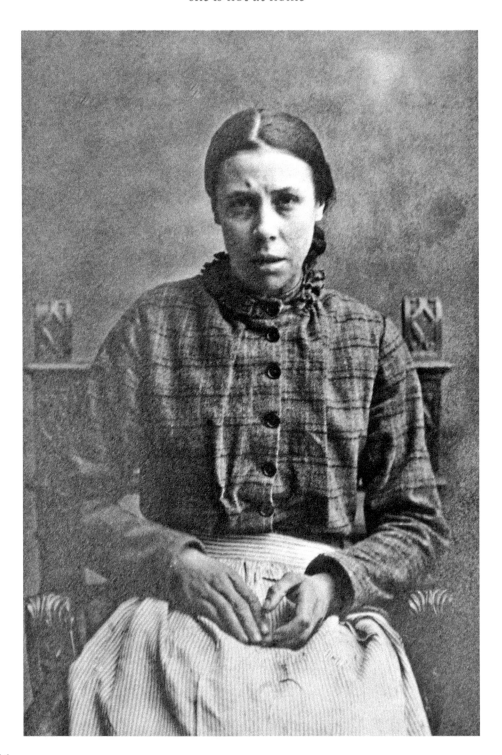

Elizabeth Hannah Martin

Number of admission: 7619

Admitted: 4 February 1909.

Age: Twenty-seven.

Age on first attack: Twenty-six.

Religious persuasion: Church of England.

Married, single or widowed: Single.

Occupation: Domestic Servant.

Chargeable to: Ripon.

Previous place of abode: 11 West Terrace, Ripon.

Name of nearest known relative: Hannah Maria Martin (mother), 11 West Terrace, Ripon.

Relatives similarly affected: A very distant relative on father's side, Elizabeth Martin (thirty years ago).

Relieving Officer: J. W. Chapleby.

Asylum: Has not been in any asylum.

Attack: First.

Insane: Three days.

Supposed cause: Not known.

Epileptic: Not.

Facts observed by W. D. Jefferson: Vacant wandering look, talks irrationally. Says she wants to go home and says her mother is not her mother and she is not at home.

Other facts communicated by Hannah Maria Martin (mother), 11 West Terrace, Ripon: Yesterday morning about 3.00 a.m. while sleeping with me, she got out of bed and rushing out of the house with very little clothing on, no stockings on and ran into a house more than a mile off (15 degrees of frost), they got her home again and at 8.00 a.m. she broke the window and got out and was held down by her brother until help was obtained.

Mental state: Very noisy and excited, resisting all attempts to soothe her. She is very restless and impulsive and throws things about. She will not eat her food and throws it at the nurse when it is brought to her. She can give a good account for herself and her memory is unimpaired.

Elizabeth was the second oldest of five children born to William and Hannah Maria Martin of Borough Bridge, North Yorkshire. Her father, who was employed as a 'Butler in service', died when Elizabeth was just three years old, in 1885. Her mother brought up the children by sewing plain shirts at home. It is not known what sparked Elizabeth's illness, but she was brought into Menston Asylum very quickly upon the onset. Within a just few months, she was noted to be quiet and well behaved whilst retaining some harmless delusions; however, unbeknown to her she was already dying of consumption (TB). When death came on 5 October 1910 at 3.45 a.m., her family failed to pick up her remains and it was left to the hospital to perform the final service.

She was buried at Buckle Lane Cemetery on 10 October 1910, row 20, grave 8.

'He looks vacantly and there is unnatural movement of hand'

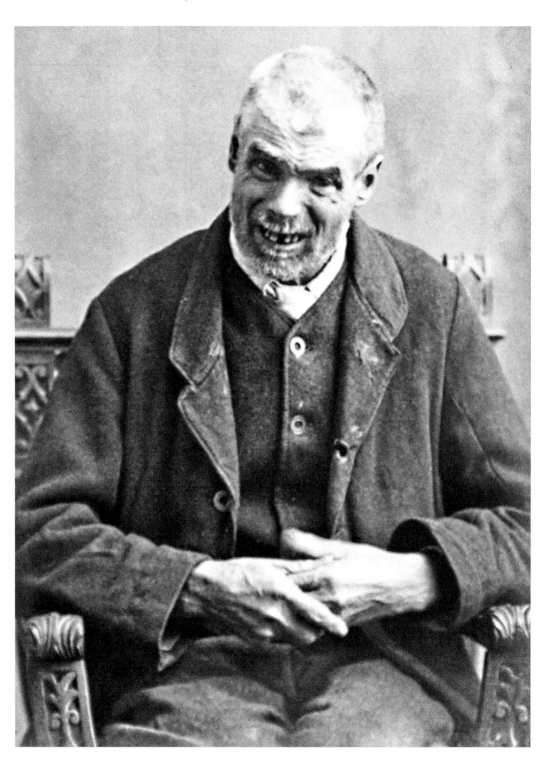

Robert Cort

Number of Admission: 421

Admitted: 13 July 1889.

Age: Thirty-nine.

Age on first attack: Thirty.

Religious persuasion: Undetermined.

Married, single or widowed: Single.

Occupation: Farmer.

Transfer from: Wakefield.

Chargeable to: Clitheroe Union.

Previous place of abode: Herbert Hall.

Name and residence of nearest known relative: Ann Cort, Herbert Hall, near Settle.

Asylum: Has not been in Wakefield Asylum.

Supposed cause: Not known.

Epileptic: Yes.

Suicidal: Not.

Dangerous to others: Yes.

Facts observed: Stupid, uncommunicative, absent, he looks vacantly and there is unnatural movement of hand.

Other facts communicated by his sister, Ann Cort: He talks and rambles to himself, never to others, swears and is defiant – laughs violently and for a long time. Is very stupid and strikes at others if interfered with.

Described as a feeble-minded epileptic with a haunted and frightened appearance, Robert would not look anyone in the face. He would cower and hide himself in the corner, away from both staff and patients. When he was photographed for the medical casebook in 1900, his continuous erratic movements made it extremely difficult to obtain a satisfactory image, such was his mental and physical condition. From the moment Robert was admitted to Menston his fate was sealed, the prognosis was unfavourable and treatment was palliative. For the thirty years Robert lived at Menston Asylum, he was incapable of any type of work, he was regarded as a much-demented epileptic although he only suffered three fits, and they were after illness. Sadly, it appears that by 1891 Robert was in deep secondary dementia, with no real understanding of his surroundings, which continued until his death in 1919.

Ninety years after his death, Robert was found by his relatives. George Appleton and his daughter Nicola, from Cumbria, now come to every open day for the memorial garden to visit Robert's grave.

He was buried at Buckle Lane Cemetery, 26 June 1919, row 23, grave 30, aged sixty-nine. Robert spent thirty years at Menston Asylum.

'She cannot give attention to work,
she is troublesome and has to be kept in seclusion'

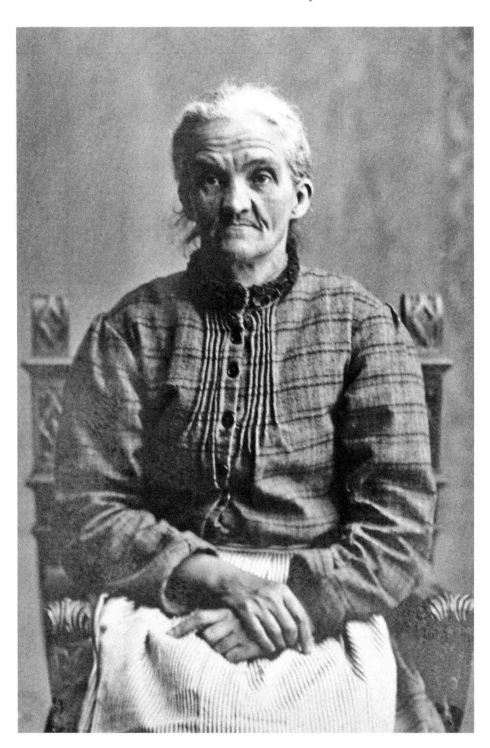

Alice Amelia Watson

Number of admission: 7761

Admitted: 26 June 1907.

Age: Sixty.

Age on first attack: Sixty.

Religious persuasion: Church of England.

Married, single or widowed: Married.

Occupation: Hawker.

Chargeable to: Leeds.

Previous place of abode: Leeds Union Workhouse Infirmary.

Name and residence of nearest known residence: Workhouse.

Relatives similarly affected: Not known.

Relieving officer: George Farrar.

Asylum: Has not been in any asylum.

Insane: Not known.

Supposed cause: Epilepsy.

Epileptic: Yes.

Suicidal: Not.

Dangerous to others: Not known.

Facts observed by J. Allan: She is childish in her conduct; she has got a large number of pictures from papers and magazines and keeps playing with them and arranging them out on her bed and about the room. She has delusions about money being left to her and wishes to go to the town hall to see about it. She makes incoherent statements about various subjects.

Other facts communicated by Harriet Roberts, Leeds Union Infirmary: Alice Amelia Watson is very restless day and night. She did stay in bed last night but walked about her room and kept singing. She cannot give attention to work, she is troublesome and has to be kept in seclusion.

Mental state: She is restless and suspicious and is very troublesome, she chatters on until she is incoherent. She objects to everything done for her.

Alice was a street hawker in that she sold goods door to door. Unfortunately, there are no census records that relate to her, so it is difficult to trace her life previous to her reception at Menston; the only record available details her death in 1919, aged seventy-two. Throughout her time at Menston, Alice's notes vary from reports that she is quarrelsome, aggressive and discontented to being quiet, tractable and employed usefully. There is, however, not one single instance of her having any epileptic fits, which was the supposed cause of her illness. At one point in 1916, Alice had to be sedated and secluded in a side room every night, as she had become refractory (resistant to treatment) and violent towards other patients.

Alice was buried at Buckle Lane Cemetery on 18 July 1919, row 23, grave 34.

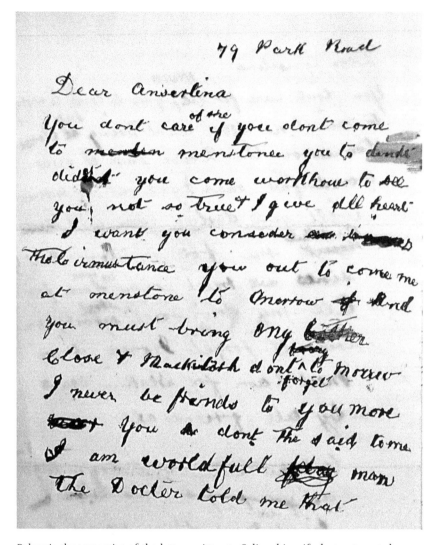

Below is the transcript of the letter written to Selina, his wife, but not posted:

Dear Anserlina, 79 Park Road

You don't care if you don't come to Menstone, you didn't come Workhouse to see, you not so true and I give you all my heart. I want you to consider the circumstance, you ought to come to me at Menstone tomorrow and you must bring any letters. I love you Mackintosh and don't forget to now, I never be friends to you more you don't, they said to me I am worldfull man the doctor told me that

William Gott

Number of admission: 2334
Admitted: 15 February 1895.
Age: Thirty.
Age on first attack: Thirty.
Religious persuasion: Church of England.
Married, single or widowed: Married.
Occupation: Railway Porter.
Chargeable to: Bradford.
Previous place of abode: Workhouse, Bradford.
Name and residence of nearest known relative: Selena Ann Gott (wife), 79 Park Road, Bradford.
Asylum: Has not been in any asylum.

Insane: One month.
Supposed cause: Not known.
Suicidal: Yes.
Dangerous to others: Yes.

Facts observed by W. B. Procter, Medical Officer at Bradford Workhouse: He is quite insane. Is very excitable at times, raves and talks incoherently, wanders about, shouts and cries and afterwards is depressed. Is sleepless at nights.

Other facts communicated by his wife, Selena A. Gott: Reports that he is very violent and dangerous at times, that he has attempted to cut his own throat, that he has also attacked her, his wife, when excited with a knife, that he raves and talks incoherently.

Mental state: Patient talks freely, but in an indistinct, emotional, incoherent manner. He has great difficulty in pronouncing linguals. Labials do not give him much trouble. His speech slow and drawling. Says he was never in better health in his life. He prides himself in his power of blacking boots. Mental capacity evidently much reduced, with speech full of adjectives. Was a soldier in the Royal Horse Artillery and has seen active service in Afghanistan. Thinks he is in the infirmary at present. When reading, he slurs over and misses words out. After finishing, he can give no idea of what he has read.

William had syphilis, which developed into general paralysis of the insane (also known as G.P.I.). The disease is characterised by mental deterioration, grandiose gestures, speech defects and progressive paralysis. An early indicator could be one pupil dilated more than the other and rash statements, such as offering anyone they meet a million pounds or a Dukedom. In 1895, there were twenty-nine deaths at Menston attributed to G.P.I., making up just over 25 per cent of all deaths in the asylum that year. The disease usually lasted around three-and-a-half years before death occurred.

William died on 31 August 1895 at 7.45 a.m. due to general paralysis of the insane. He was buried at Buckle Lane Cemetery on 5 September 1895, row 17, grave 19.

'She stands on her head and sings ribald songs'

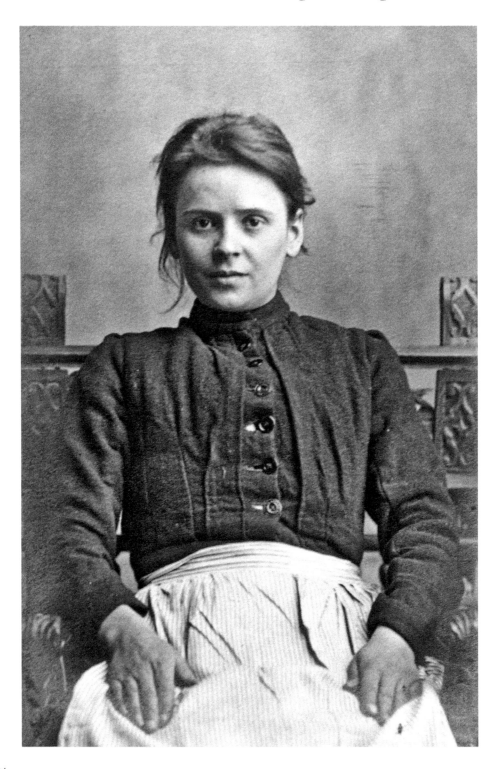

Mabel Grey

Number of Admission: 8387
Admitted: 3 June 1909.
Occupation: Housewife.
Age: Twenty-eight.
Age on first attack: Twenty-seven.
Married, single or widowed: Married.
Previous place of abode: Bradford Union Workhouse Infirmary.
Nearest known relative: Outhwaite Fearnside (father), 14 Glendare Road, Bradford.
Religious persuasion: Wesleyan Methodist.
Relieving Officer: W. O. Mackley.
Relatives similarly affected: None.

Insane: Ten days.
Supposed cause: Husband's conduct.
Suicidal: Not known.
Dangerous to others: Yes.

Facts observed by B. H. Slater: She talks constantly, incoherently and irrationally, skipping lightly from one subject to another. She weeps at times without cause. She has no memory for recent events.

Other facts communicated by Selina Charlesworth from Bradford Union Workhouse: She is very noisy and fretful. She talks irrationally and she is always interfering with other patients.

Mental state: She talks incessantly and incoherently and takes no interest when spoken to. She is violent and destructive and stands at the door all day and night banging on the walls and the door. She stands on her head and sings ribald songs (a bawdy song is a humorous song which emphasises sexual themes and is often rich with innuendo). She is quite irrational and extremely restless.

Mabel was admitted to Menston in June 1909, diagnosed with Chronic Mania. The term 'mania' was a Victorian favourite when it came to diagnosing people entering the asylum (the definition of mania is 'to rage furiously'). The supposed cause of Mabel's illness was determined to be 'conflict with husband'; the reality was that she had been infected with syphilis. We will never know if it was her husband who infected Mabel – the disease would kill her regardless. With this disease, remission is extremely rare, however Mabel was discharged, improved, on 15 September 1915. This was short-lived, as she was to return soon after, and died aged twenty-nine on 25 November 1910 at 6.45 a.m., in the presence of Nurse Wilkinson.

It was only after her post-mortem that the cause of death was determined as general paralysis of the insane. General paralysis of the insane (G.P.I.) was one of the most devastating diseases observed in British psychiatry during the nineteenth century after 1840, in terms of the high number and type of patients diagnosed, the severity of its symptoms and, above all, its utterly hopeless prognosis.

Mabel was buried at Buckle Lane Cemetery on 30 November 1910, row 20, grave 13.

'He has delusions that he is going to be hung and also to be smothered'

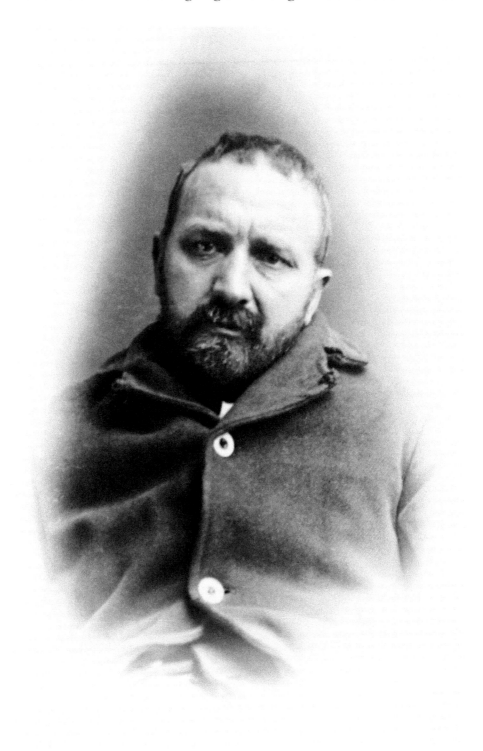

George Brewer

Number of admission: 213

Admitted: 1 February 1889.

Age: Twenty-nine.

Age on first attack: Twenty-seven.

Religious persuasion: Church of England.

Married, single or widowed: Married.

Occupation: Pot Hawker.

Chargeable to: Bradford.

Previous place of abode: Bradford Union Workhouse Infirmary.

Name and residence of nearest known relative: Emma Brewer, 231 Back Lane, Bowling, Bradford.

History: A transfer from Wadsley Asylum, into which he was admitted 17 February 1887. Tried to cut his own throat with scissors. Generally drunk on a Saturday and a Sunday.

Facts observed by W. B. Proctor F.R.C.S., Bradford, 1 Feb 1889: He is quite insane and has many delusions: that his wife does not regard him, that he has thousands of enemies, that they are on the lookout to shoot him, etc. Is dangerous to himself, tries to choke himself with his fingers and in eating his food. Tries to get out of the window.

Other facts communicated by his stepmother, Mary Ann Holdsworth: He has been ill for nine or ten weeks, but out of his mind for five weeks. He has delusions that he is going to be hung and also to be smothered. He has refused his food and has become sleepless at nights.

Mental state: Patient has a wretched, miserable appearance. Makes not the slightest response to external stimulation beyond a surly, obstinate and vicious resistance, even at an attempt to cut his face.

Suicidal: Yes.

Dangerous to others: Yes.

Diagnosis: Chronic mania.

Causation: Not ascertained.

Prognosis: Unfavourable.

Treatment: Nil.

Diagnosis mania, prognosis unfavourable, George did not stand a chance. He was there for life and there was not the slightest intention to treat him – this was simply custodial care. Although regarded as useful in the ward, George had dementia, which was apparently a result of alcohol abuse. By September 1909, his memory had quite gone and was unable to identify the day of the week. He believed the year to be 1925.

George was never to see 1925, for he died in January 1914, aged fifty-four. The apparent cause of death was valvular disease of the heart, which was ascertained by post-mortem.

He was buried at Buckle Lane Cemetery on 25 January 1914, row 28, grave 16. George spent twenty-seven years at Menston Asylum.

'Since the age of twenty he has been in the habit of drinking heavily'

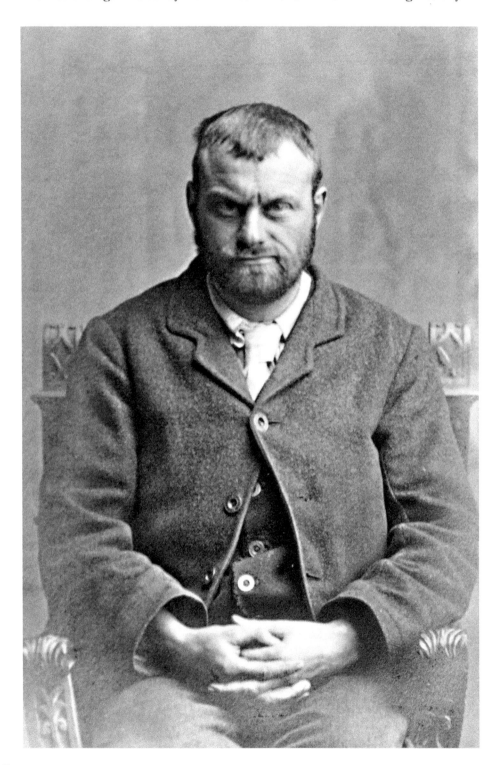

Ernest Austin

Number of admission: 7727
Admitted: 30 May 1907.
Age: Twenty-seven.
Age at first attack: Twenty-seven.
Religious persuasion: Church of England.
Married, single or widowed: Single.
Occupation: Dyer.
Chargeable to: Bradford.
Previous place of abode: Bradford Union Workhouse.
Name and residence of nearest known relative: Willie Austin (father), 204 City Road, Bradford.
Relatives similarly affected: Maternal uncle, George Brewer, in Menston Asylum for the last twenty years.
Asylum: Has not been in any asylum.

Insane: Four days.
Supposed cause: Drink.
Epileptic: Not.
Suicidal: Yes.
Dangerous to others: Yes.

History: An uncle of his has been a patient here for some years. Since the age of twenty, he has been in the habit of drinking heavily. He has a childish look and does not appear to be able to grasp anything that is said to him. In his earlier life he was bright and intelligent. There appears to have been a steady failure of all the mental faculties. He is excited and restless. Has to be put in the side room at night, throws himself about if opportunity presents itself. He has auditory hallucinations and whistling and ringing of bells. Has a delusion that he is filled with electricity. He often mistakes identity.

Ernest arrived at Menston twenty years after his maternal uncle, George Brewer, who we met on page 77. Just like his uncle, Ernest's problem related to intemperance (alcohol abuse), and he was also diagnosed with mania. Initially, Ernest was quite depressed and his memory impaired, but he did manage to do some work on the ward. By June 1910, it was noted in his file that he 'has improved considerably during the last few months and though still confused, he is able to answer questions rationally. He is much brighter – works well in the ward. Bodily health is very satisfactory.'

Given his vast improvement, it is then surprising that instead of potentially being released as relieved, he was instead kept at Menston for a further fifty years. From being admitted as a young man in his twenties, Ernest saw two World Wars and the transition from lunatic asylum to mental hospital before he died in 1960, aged eighty. There would be 106 more burials at Buckle Lane before it closed after Ernest was laid to rest, 17 rows and 17 graves away from his uncle George. Ernest and his uncle, George, clocked up eighty years between them as patients.

Ernest was buried at Buckle Lane Cemetery on 30 May 1960, row 11, grave 33. He spent fifty-three years at Menston Asylum.

'She gathers bits of bread and calls them her baby'

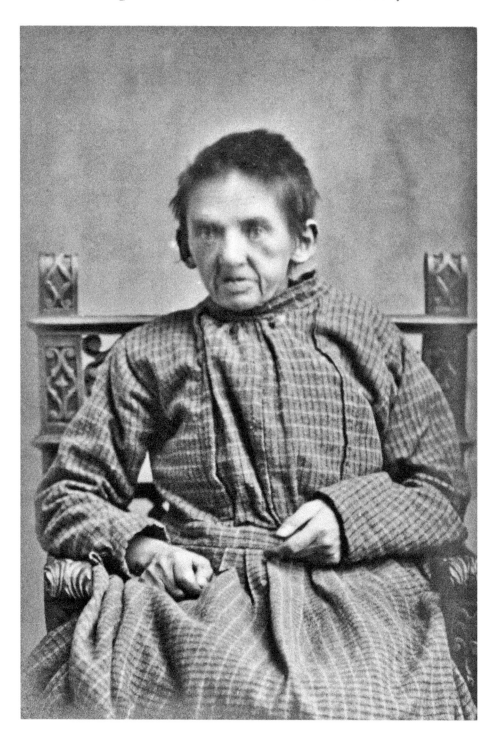

Lavinia Berry

Number of admission: 9012

Admitted: 3 February 1911.

Age: Fifty.

Age on first attack: Not known.

Religious persuasion: Church of England.

Married, single or widowed: Married.

Occupation: Mill hand.

Chargeable to: Bradford.

Previous place of abode: Bradford Union Workhouse.

Nearest known relative: Not known.

Relieving Officer: Alfred Wood.

Insane: Four days.

Supposed cause: Not known.

Epileptic: Yes.

Suicidal: Yes.

Dangerous to others: Yes.

Facts observed by B. H. Slater: She wanders about wildly waving her arms or clamping her apron to her breast and says 'this is my baby, twelve months old'. She gathers bits of bread and calls them her baby as well. She has erotic tendencies.

Other facts communicated by Fanny Slater, Attendant, Bradford Workhouse: She is very destructive, restless and annoys other patients by pushing them out of bed at night. She has put her head under the hot water tap.

Mental condition: Patient is in a condition of marked restlessness, moving about, and will not remain quiet for a moment. She is noisy and incoherent and will not reply to questions put to her and resents any interference. She pays little attention to her surroundings and does not appear to realise where she is.

From the moment Lavinia arrived at Menston, it was clear her prognosis was bleak. Dr Samuel Edgerley, the medical superintendent, wasted no time in sending her to the female chronic block just one week after her reception. Described as withered and poorly nourished, she also had a weak pulse according to her notes.

By July the same year, Lavinia was failing both mentally and physically and passed away just one month later on 19 August 2011 at 12.15 p.m., in the presence of Nurse Bradley.

Cause of death was ascertained as general paralysis of the insane by way of post-mortem.

Lavinia was buried at Buckle Lane Cemetery on 23 August 1911, row 21, grave 15.

'He states that he saw the devil come out of the dawn and
dance round the light'

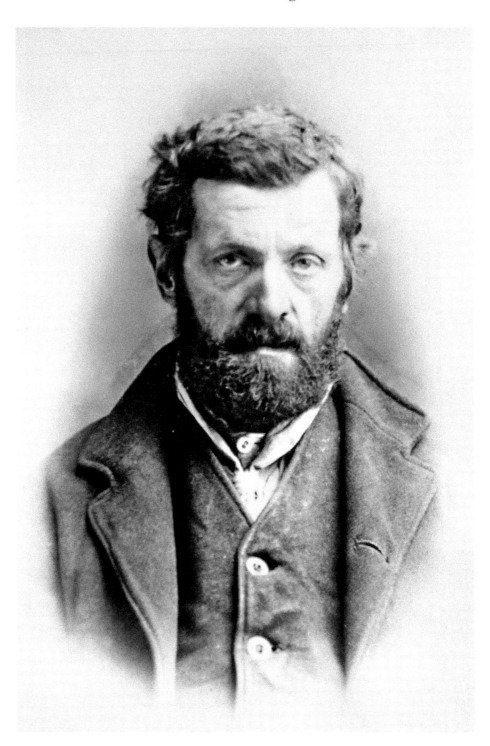

Joseph Dewhirst

Number of admission: 149
Admitted: 22 December 1888.
Age: Thirty.
Age on first attack: Twenty-one.
Religious persuasion: Independent.
Married, single or widowed: Single.
Transfer from: Wakefield.
Nearest relative: Brother, 78 Well Street, Wilsden.

Facts observed by P. S. Coyan M.D.: He has told me he wished to drown himself. He states that he saw the devil come out of the dawn and dance round the light. He talks incoherently on various subjects and he says a mad dog licked his face and worried the words out of his mouth. He says the bad man was working in his side and stopped him from following his employment.

Other facts communicated: He thinks that his sins cannot be forgiven. He talks of drowning himself. He is sleepless and talks incoherently night and day.

History: A transfer from Wakefield Asylum into which he was admitted upon a certificate dated 22 September 1879.

Mental state: Patient is hopelessly lost and incoherent, if a little mildly excited. His flow of conversation is so marked that it requires a little attention to discern that there is nothing of relevance in it. It is quite impossible to get a rational or pertinent reply from him.

Diagnosis: Chronic mania.
Prognosis: Unfavourable.
Treatment: Nil.
Epileptic: Yes.

When Joseph arrived at Menston Asylum, he had already completed eleven years as a patient at the Wakefield Asylum. Upon his reception at Menston, he was immediately diagnosed as chronically ill with dementia. When spoken to, his conversation, although irrational, focussed on his previous life prior to certification. He believed he had only just arrived, and was unaware of his surroundings. Joseph was regarded as a good worker, especially in mechanical employments, and had a multitude of jobs at the hospital over the years, including working in the chip house, the hair shop and the boiler house.

It is not known what sins he believed were unforgivable. The only record of Joseph's life prior to admission relates to 1871 when, aged thirteen, he was employed as a spinner in the mill and lived with his widowed father, John, sister Elizabeth and three brothers.

When Joseph passed away in 1929, he had spent half a century under care and treatment.

He was buried at Buckle Lane Cemetery on 10 June 1929, row 22, grave 16.

'Fancies that she hears voices telling her that her husband is being cut into pieces'

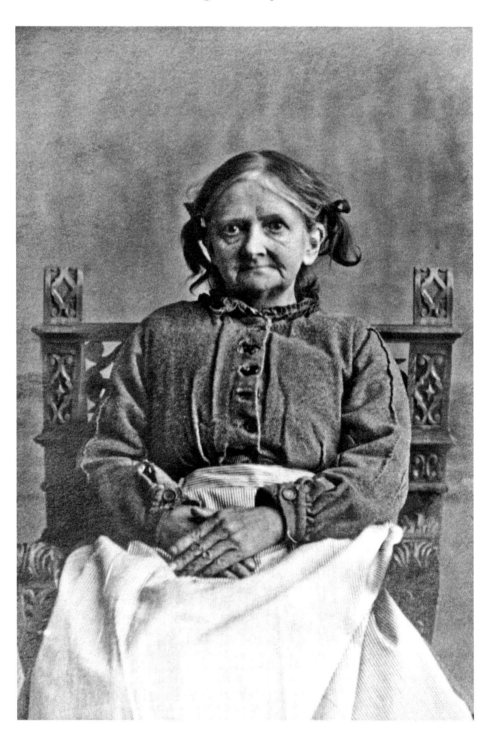

Elizabeth Scholfield

Number of admission: 8282

Admitted: 25 January 1909.

Age: Sixty-two.

Age on first attack: Sixty-two.

Married, single or widowed: Widow.

Occupation: Housewife.

Religious persuasion: Church of England.

Chargeable to: North Bierley.

Previous place of abode: Bradford Union Workhouse Infirmary, Clayton.

Nearest known relative: Jonas Holmes, 2 Church Yard, Kildwick.

Relatives similarly affected: Not known.

Relieving Officer: J. Hughes.

Facts observed by W. Cunliffe: She is very excitable, shouting and swearing. She imagines that the police are coming to fetch her for some crime. She states that I am the cause of her body being charged with electricity. She is constantly hearing imaginary voices and seeing people that are not present.

Other facts communicated by Annie R. Hare, nurse in the infirmary, Clayton, Bradford: Scholfield fancies that she hears voices telling her that her husband is being cut into pieces and that her food is being poisoned. She is very excitable, wanders up and down and uses very bad language.

Mental state: She is very noisy and excited, quarrelling with everyone, very restless and troublesome. She suffers from auditory hallucinations and addresses people who are not present. She requires a great deal of attention.

Elizabeth, upon her reception to Menston, was immediately regarded as a troublemaker who refused work. By the end of 1909, the medical superintendent, Samuel Edgerley, sealed her fate by sending her to the female chronic block. On 10 February 1910, it was noted on her medical record, 'Patient was pushed against the edge of a door by another patient and hit the top of her right shoulder yesterday. There is a swelling about the size of a tangerine orange and is very painful.'

This injury was to kill Elizabeth, for it was further noted on 7 March 1910, 'She continues to have high temperatures at night. The wound is discharging and shows no tendency to heal. The movements of the joint are painful and fluid is apparent in the discharge.' And again on 14 March 1910: 'She is losing strength and the condition of the shoulder does not improve. It is increasingly painful and there is evident erosion of bone. Her temperature continues high and her pulse is very feeble.' Elizabeth passed away on 26 March at 8.40 a.m., in the presence of Nurse Shepherd. The cause of death, which was ascertained by post-mortem, was attributed to atrophy of the brain and her shoulder injury. Although only a patient for just over a year, there was no one to collect Elizabeth's remains.

She was buried at Buckle Lane Cemetery on 31 March 1910, row 18, grave 17.

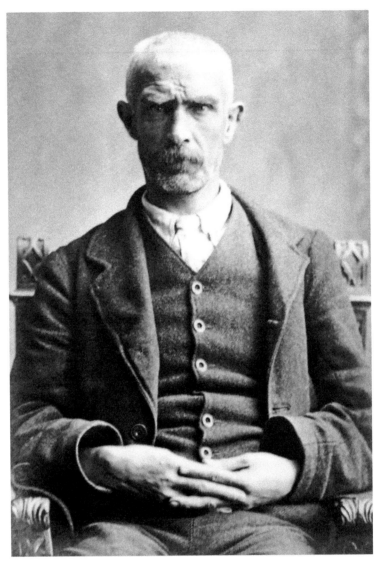

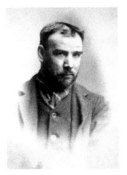 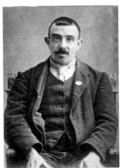 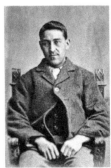

James Knott

Number of admission: 6578.

Admitted: 7 March 1904.

Age: Thirty-three.

Age on first attack: Thirty-three.

Religious persuasion: Church of England.

Married, single or widowed: Married.

Occupation: Stoker.

Chargeable to: North Bierley.

Previous place of abode: North Bierley Union Workhouse, Clayton.

Name and residence of nearest known relative: Mary Knott, Denholme, near Bradford.

Asylum: Has not been in any asylum.

Facts observed by J. Jackson, 5 March 1904: He is stupid and unable to talk coherently, especially after an epileptic attack. He is dangerous to other inmates. He has made some attempts to run away from the workhouse.

Other facts communicated by Thomas Dodds, male attendant, Clayton Workhouse, Bradford: He is dangerous to other inmates by making violent attacks upon them and he threatens to escape and has done so.

Mental state: This patient readily engages in conversation and is able to give some account of his past life, but is childish and fatuous in his manner, and exhibits little knowledge of the fitness of things. He gives a history of recent epilepsy and admits that he has no knowledge of his actions about the period of his epileptic attacks. At present, he is quiet and tractable and has some limited knowledge of and interest in his surroundings.

Insane: Four months.

Epileptic: Yes.

Dangerous to others: Yes.

Diagnosis: Dementia.

Cause: Epilepsy.

Prognosis: Not favourable.

Treatment: Nil.

Things looked bad for James when admitted to Menston in 1904. By all accounts, he was stupid, childish and a demented epileptic – the prognosis was distinctly unfavourable. Described as both quiet and tractable, yet at the same time violent and dangerous, James was going nowhere; well, not until 7 December 1906 when it was noted, 'This patient, along with three others, yesterday afternoon escaped from the asylum at about 3.45 p.m. He was out exercising in the airing court where he scaled the railings after leaving the urinal where he was in hiding. He got away and was absent the whole of the evening and the night.' James was soon recaptured, along with his fellow escapees pictured below James (page 80).

The quartet's remarkable adventure was fully reported in the Bradford Daily Telegraph *and is fully transcribed on the following pages.*

Once recaptured, James remained at Menston until his death on April fool's day, 1918. The apparent cause of death was epilepsy; his death certificate was signed by Dr Richard Kirwan.

James was buried at Buckle Lane Cemetery on 6 April 1918, row 16, grave 40, aged forty-eight.

It is hard to believe that such an apparently demented patient who, if we trust his notes, struggled to function on a basic level, could make such an escape. If we believe James notes to be exaggerated, then where does it leave every other patient in this book?

Bradford Daily Telegraph, 7 December 1906.

LUNATICS AT LARGE

ESCAPE FROM MENSTON ASYLUM

HUNT BY POLICE AND WARDERS

THREE FUGITIVES CAUGHT AT HAWORTH

During the night, Bingley, Keighley and the surrounding districts have been the scene of an exciting hunt after four escaped lunatics.

The quartet succeeded in gaining liberty from detention at Menston Asylum and made their way through Baildon and Shipley to Bingley.

How they effected their escape is at present a mystery, but it is reported that, being quiet patients, they were allowed considerable licence whilst at exercise in the grounds late yesterday afternoon.

Finding themselves unobserved they walked away, and once outside the grounds they took to flight, making their destination the Worth Valley, where it is supposed one of the lunatics hails from.

Their escape was soon discovered and warders were immediately sent out to scour the countryside and one of the warders was sent forward on a bicycle to inform the police authorities at Shipley.

Notwithstanding these precautions the fugitives managed to pass through both Baildon and Shipley in daylight, undetected.

This is somewhat strange considering the fact that all the men were dressed in the regulation inmates garb, consisting of dark tweed suits branded 'Menston Asylum', shirts and stockings with red bands on the top, and black buckled boots.

On hearing of the matter, a *Telegraph* representative immediately made inquiries at Menston Asylum, but the authorities were very reticent, but confessed that an escape had been effected, and that the warders were in stern pursuit.

Subsequently, however, our representative ascertained that the men's names and descriptions were as follows:-

James Knott, 44 years of age, five feet nine inches in height and of dark complexion.

Walter Longbottom, 40 years of age, 4ft 6in. in height, dark hair turning grey.

Charles Tillotson, 26 years of age, 5ft 6in. in height, dark complexion with slight moustache.

Charles Frederick Sutcliffe, 26 years of age, 5ft 6in. high of light complexion.

After leaving Shipley, the men – who evidently separated – made their way through Nab Wood and along the Bradford Road.

Just before reaching Messrs W. R. and R. Atkinson's joinery works at Bingley, they narrowly escaped capture through the keen observation of Police Constable Hardy. This officer saw a man of diminutive stature – evidently Longbottom – behaving in a suspicious manner. He was ambling along in a peculiar manner, and behaving with pronounced eccentricity. His suspicions aroused, he followed the man and passed close by him at Messrs. Atkinsons' works.

Longbottom, noticing he was observed, doubled into the road and walked quickly on, re-passing the policeman. On reaching the Kings Head Hotel, the man was joined by another, and the two walked together into Myrtle Place, where they joined two others.

Hardy – who it should be mentioned did not know that lunatics were at large – turned down Myrtle Pace to the Police Station.

He looked around, and saw the four men standing by Mr Butterfield's shop watching him.

Immediately they realised that he had again seen them they made off down Main Street in the direction of Keighley.

The news of the escape from Menston was shortly afterwards conveyed to the police authorities at Bingley, and Hardy, who immediately suspicioned the men he had seen as being the persons wanted, set off on a bicycle in the direction of Keighley.

He was assisted by Police Constable Mobbs, who proceeded on foot to Sandbeds.

In the meantime, the police at Keighley were notified of the approach of the suspected pedestrians, and elaborate arrangements were made to affect their capture by means of a cordon.

Hardy's efforts to overtake the men were unsuccessful, though it was afterwards ascertained from a Bradford carrier that the fugitives had been seen at Sandbeds.

The men must have had a suspicion that the police authorities at Keighley had been informed of their approach, and they then struck across country in the direction of the Worth Valley.

A keen lookout was maintained by the police throughout the night, and early this morning, three of the escaped men – Knott, Longbottom, and Sutcliffe – were captured at Haworth.

The arrests were made quietly, for the men apparently realised the futility of resistance.

The officers bringing about the capture were Sergeant Lambert and Police Constable Clarke of the West Riding Constabulary.

The whereabouts of Tillotson were at the time unknown.

The prisoners were conveyed to the Keighley Police Station where they will be detained until an escort of warders arrives to convey them back to the asylum.

Bradford Daily Telegraph, 8 December 1906.

THE ESCAPED LUNATICS, AMUSING INCIDENT AT KEIGHLEY

The report that the four lunatics who escaped from Menston Asylum yesterday sought to evade the police by striking across country from Sandbeds, appears to have been incorrect. They appear to have proceeded via Stockbridge to Keighley.

An amusing incident in connection with their visit is that immediately on arrival in Keighley they went into Turner's hairdressing rooms near the station and requested the barber to shave them. From the conduct of the men the barber was suspicious, but it was not until shaving the last man that he felt convinced of the insanity of his customers.

He questioned the last man to be shaved as to where he came from, and he was informed that the quartet had walked from Menston that day. 'Have you been working there?' inquired the barber, and the reply was 'yes; working a whole week for three half ounces of shag; we're sick of it and we're determined not to stand it any longer.'

The men then went out of the shop, and proceeded through Keighley. The barber confessed that he was thankful that he had not known the character of his customers from the first, for if they had been at all violent disposed the array of razors might have tempted them.

The man, Tillotson, is still at large, and it is thought he is somewhere upon the hills overlooking the Worth Valley.

Bradford Daily Telegraph, 14 December 1906.

THE ESCAPED LUNATICS

THE FOURTH CAPTURED

All the four lunatics who escaped from Menston Asylum have now been accounted for.

Three were returned to their quarters on Friday, but the fourth, a man named Tillotson, was not taken till Saturday morning.

He was a native of Oakworth, and the warders and police naturally surmised that he would make for his home. Nor were they surprised, for the house was watched, and Tillotson was seen to approach. He was taken quietly by the warders and removed to Menston Asylum.

Our Menston correspondent writes: The last of the men who escaped from Menston Asylum, Charles Tillotson, was taken back to the asylum shortly before one o' clock on Saturday and they were interviewed by the doctor of the asylum. The men were asked the reason why they went away, and they replied that they wanted a day off to see their friends. They went by way of Baildon, Saltaire and Bingley and Tillotson was standing in front of a newsagent's shop on Friday at Keighley, and saw a placard announcing that madmen were at large. A policeman came up to him and said, 'It's a bad do about these madmen getting away' and Tillotson replied, 'Yes, it is: but I think they will be glad to get back again. I don't think they will do anyone any harm.' And the policeman said, 'I don't know so much about that; we want to get hold of them.' Tillotson then went away and visited several friends in Keighley, and finally went to his mother's at Oakworth, where he was captured, and was brought back to the Asylum on Saturday morning.

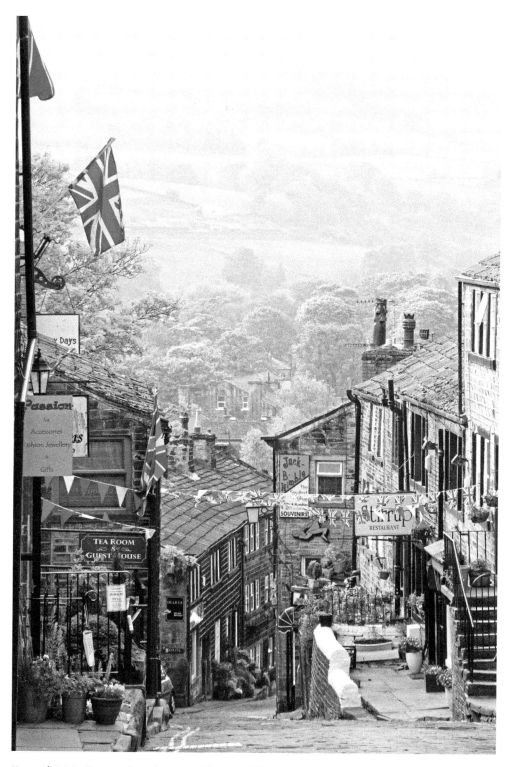

Haworth Main Street, where James and his two fellow escapees were caught before being returned to Menston.

'She has threatened injury to younger children in the house'

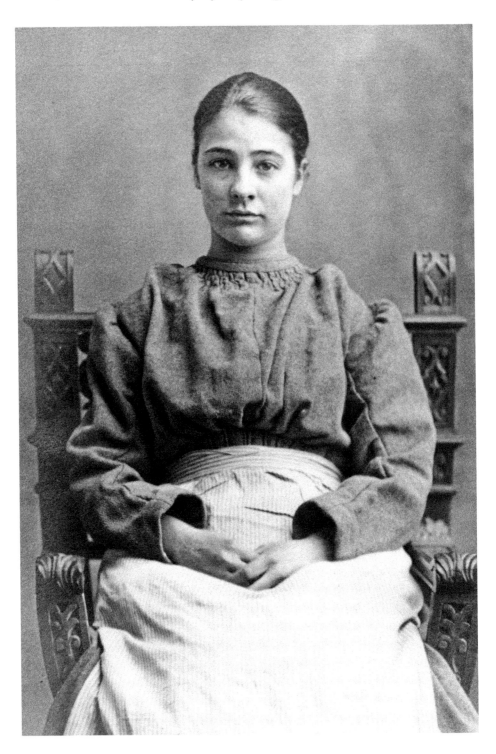

Ada Ward

Number of admission: 9035
Admitted: 14 July 1911.
Age: Nineteen.
Age on first attack: Nineteen.
Married, single or widowed: Single.
Occupation: Spinner.
Chargeable to: North Bierley.
Previous place of abode: 26 Robin Lane.
Nearest known relative: Ben Ward (father), 26 Robin Lane, Pudsey.

Insane: Three weeks.
Supposed cause: Not known.
Suicidal: Yes.
Dangerous to others: Yes.

Facts observed by H. Kershaw: On interviewing her she was abusive and would not answer questions and ordered me out of the house and then suddenly burst into a fit of laughter. She would not allow anyone to approach her and when not talking was muttering incoherently to herself.

Other facts communicated by Susan Ward, her mother, living at home address: She cannot leave her alone as she has threatened injury to younger children in the house. She had the greatest difficulty in stopping her from putting her head in the fire. She is constantly talking to herself and suddenly without cause bursting into fits of laughter or crying.

Mental state: Patient will not engage in conversations and is very resistant to examination, mental or physical. She is childish and irrational in her manner, laughing and crying without any cause. She appears to have no knowledge of her surroundings and has no sense of responsibility for her actions.

On the 1911 census, Ada's name has been crossed out with just two small notes added: 'at the asylum' and 'feeble minded'. Ada was the daughter of Ben (a labourer) and Susan Ward. She was the second eldest of five daughters; the youngest, Annie, was seven years old when Ada was admitted. The Wards had seven children in total, however, on the census it states that two had died already by 1911.

Entering the asylum at just nineteen years old, Ada was regarded as hysterical and silly by medical staff. The only improvement noted was on 12 November 1911: 'Has shown some mental improvement and is more natural in her conversation. She is now working steadily in the laundry though still very simple and childish.' In 1914, she was sent to the chronic block where she would live out her days for the next half a century. Ada died in September 1967, aged seventy-five years old. She saw the transition from pauper lunatic asylum to mental hospital in the 1920s, and finally High Royds Psychiatric Hospital in the early 1960s.

She was laid to rest at Buckle Lane Cemetery, row 13, grave 27, on 8 September 1967.

There was only to be eleven more burials before the cemetery finally closed in January 1969.

"Hamlet's Soliloquy on Life and Death"
As an Improvement.
By John Denton.

1. From the sun's uprising beam—toward the West
I turn my steps unto a known retreat
On my left hand; and entering its portal—
On my right behold a cart-wide-open room
Of some ten-eight yards extent: A blustering throng
Of fete-enjoying folk within; their motions seen,
I then would have proceeded on my errand bound
Further toward the south on business bent:
But looking in the open, and pressing on—
My slipping feet essaying to proceed,
Methinks the room did slide within from south,
Exhibiting the high Lord and Majesty of the place
Demanding evidence of my regal right
To appear, and not before Him exempt
Of drossy matter on the earth domains:

To be, or not to be,—that is the question:
Whether 'tis nobler in the mind to suffer
The slings and arrows of outrageous fortune,
Or to take arms against a Sea of troubles
And, by opposing, end them?—To die,—to sleep!

2. My pained bones upheaved my shoulder & from
My still more smarting heart, prevading a
sleepy exhaustion caused me to desist
From reading off my character as felt

No more. And by a sleep to say we end
The heart-ache, and a thousand natural shocks

John Denton

Number of admission: 167
Admitted: 22 December 1888.
Age: Fifty-nine.
Age on first attack: Thirty.
Religious persuasion: Wesleyan Methodist.
Married, single or widowed: Single.
Occupation: Letter Press, Printer.
Chargeable to: Bradford.
Transfer from: Wakefield.
Previous place of abode: Bradford.
Name and residence of nearest relative: Charles Denton (brother), Low Bridge, Bradford.

Facts observed: Cannot converse rationally on any subject for any length of time – imagines everyone has a dislike of him and turns away from him when they see him. Told me that he ran away from Lord Palmerston as soon as he saw him.

Other facts communicated: For some years, he has been rather 'soft' – this has been gradually increasing. He loses himself in conversation. Imagines everyone hates him. Writing ridiculous letters to the mayor and other people.

Supposed cause: Not known.
Dangerous to others: Yes.

John was a poet, although the medical staff thought not. It mattered not, for it brought John great comfort when times were tough and I suppose that is all that mattered at the time. Described as childish, he was, however, happy and contented, his poetry absorbing all his time and thoughts. He believed himself to be the finest poet the world had seen and rewrote 'Hamlet's soliloquy on Life and Death' as an improvement, as seen on the following page.

John passed away on 17 February 1896, aged sixty-seven, from tuberculosis, and was buried at Buckle Lane Cemetery five days later, row 17, grave 18.

It is both fitting and pertinent that the last voice in this book comes from John.

'Hamlet's soliloquy on Life and Death', as an improvement by John Denton

From the sun's uprising beam toward the west
I turn my steps unto a known retreat
On my left hand; and entering its portal
On my right behold a cart wide open room
Of some ten eighty and extent: a blustering throng
Of fête enjoying folk within; their motions seen
I then would have proceeded on my errand bound
Twither toward the south on business bent
But looking in the open and pressing on
My slipping feet saying to proceed
Me thinks the room did slide within from south
Exhibiting the high lord and the majesty of the place
Demanding evidence of my regal right
To appear and not before Him exult
Of dropsy matter on the earth domains

To be or not to be – that is the question
Whether tis nobler in the mind to suffer
The slings and arrows of outrageous fortune
Or to take arms against a sea of troubles
And by opposing, end them, to die – to sleep.
My pained bones upheaved my shoulder from
My still ness Harding heart, pervading a
Sleepy exhaustion caused me to desist
From reading off my character as felt

No more. And by a sleep to say we end
The heartache and a thousand natural shocks.

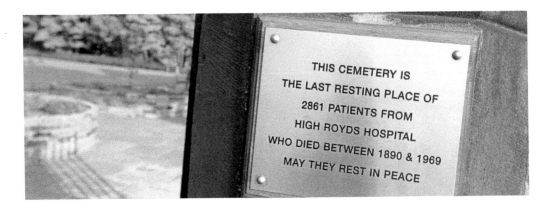

THIS CEMETERY IS
THE LAST RESTING PLACE OF
2861 PATIENTS FROM
HIGH ROYDS HOSPITAL
WHO DIED BETWEEN 1890 & 1969
MAY THEY REST IN PEACE